THE
UNDISCOVERED CONTINENT

Suzanne Juhasz

THE
UNDISCOVERED
CONTINENT

Emily Dickinson and the
Space of the Mind

INDIANA UNIVERSITY PRESS · *Bloomington*

Manufactured in the United States of America

Library of Congress Cataloging in Publication Data

Juhasz, Suzanne, 1942–
The undiscovered continent.

Bibliography: p.
Includes index.
1. Dickinson, Emily, 1830–1886—Criticism and
interpretation. 2. Imagination. 3. Solitude.
4. Feminism and literature. I. Title.
PS1541.Z5J8   1984   811'.4   82-49014
ISBN 0-253-36164-8
1 2 3 4 5 87 86 85 84 83

For my daughters: Alexandra, Jennifer, and Antonia

CONTENTS

ACKNOWLEDGMENTS

Over the six-year period in which I was writing this book, many colleagues, students, and friends have helped me to think about Emily Dickinson in increasingly interesting ways. I am especially appreciative of the scholarship of Charles Anderson, Sandra Gilbert and Susan Gubar, Margaret Homans, Karl Keller, Barbara Mossberg, and Robert Weisbuch. My debt to Josephine Miles is profound. Her response to my work has been criticism in the highest sense: astute, revelatory, challenging. I am grateful to have been her student and to continue as her companion in the profession.

Special thanks go to my three daughters, Alexandra, Jennifer, and Antonia, always a source of love and encouragement.

I am indebted to the American Association of University Women, who awarded me a fellowship in 1981–1982. A sabbatical leave from the University of Colorado and a grant-in-aid from its Council on Research and Creative Work were also important forms of assistance. My thanks to Colleen Anderson, Carolyn Dameron, and Marjorie Urban, who typed the manuscript beautifully.

Finally, my words of appreciation must include some reference to Dickinson herself, for being such an exhilarating subject. It has been a persistent pleasure to have spent so much time in her company.

Portions of this book in earlier versions were published in *The Missouri Review, Ball State University Forum, Massachusetts Studies in English,* and *The American Transcendental Quarterly.*

i *"The Landscape of the Spirit"*

Soto! Explore thyself!
Therein thyself shalt find
The "Undiscovered Continent" –
No Settler had the Mind.
[832]*

1

THE "UNDISCOVERED CONTINENT" is one of Emily Dickinson's descriptions of the mind. Another, from a letter to her friend Mrs. Holland, is "the Landscape of the Spirit."¹ Poem and prose statement indicate both the centrality of her exploration of self and also how the place where it occurred, the mind, is conceived of as actual, substantial, there. "Continent," "Landscape"—these words grant spatial dimension to the mind, the setting for Dickinson's most significant experience.

In this book I take literally Dickinson's assessment of the mind as tangible space. I am concerned with how she defines the mind as a place in which to live and with what happens to her, living there. First I look at the place, the mind, as her poems reveal it. Next I study the poetic language she creates in order to talk about mental experience. Then I focus upon three examples of intensest, extremest mental experience—pain, delight, and eternity—and show how her constructs of language enact, understand, and control significant experience. Finally I discuss the implications of Dickinson's choice of solitude, for her and for women in our own time.

The fact that Dickinson lived primarily in the mind is not a new observation. It has long been acknowledged as a factor central to her

*Texts of the poems are from *The Poems of Emily Dickinson,* edited by Thomas H. Johnson (Cambridge: The Belknap Press of Harvard University Press, 1955).

1

biography and to her art. Yet critics of Dickinson have interpreted the situation variously. In particular, there is a radical difference of perspective, and opinion, on this subject between feminist critics and traditional critics that is based in their understanding of gender.

Traditional criticism frequently begins with the assumption that Dickinson's move into the mind was a retreat. For example, George Whicher, in his "classic" biography, *This Was a Poet,* sees her reclusiveness as a self-imprisonment occasioned by a failed love affair (his vote goes to Charles Wadsworth, among the several candidates proposed over the years). "Only a Robert Browning could have released the Lady of Shalott, and no Robert Browning came her way." Her unhappiness in love, which he labels "a death blow to her heart," turns into "a life blow to her mind," so that her poetry, the result of living in that mind, is seen as compensatory activity: "Perhaps as a poet she could find the fulfillment she had missed as a woman."[2]

John Cody, whose *After Great Pain: The Inner Life of Emily Dickinson* is psychoanalytic in orientation, takes Whicher's position even further. He labels Dickinson's retreat into the mind madness, a "psychotic breakdown" occasioned by her "sexual bewilderment, anxiety and frustration," which in turn was caused by her mother's "failure as a sufficiently loving and admirable developmental model." Because Dickinson could not emulate her mother, she experienced, says Cody, strong identification with her father and later, her brother. It was this abnormal masculine identification that "although blocking her completion as a woman, stimulated her to use her mind." This ongoing abnormality—she never settled into either a "thoroughgoing and 'mature' masculine identification" or a female one—gave rise to, in his opinion, her latent homosexuality, sexual terror, and general craziness; *but,* he announced, "The point, important for American literature, is that threatening personality disintegration compelled a frantic Emily Dickinson to create poetry—for her a psychosis-deflecting activity."[3]

A study as recent as David Porter's 1981 *Dickinson: The Modern Idiom* also considers the famous "withdrawal" to be responsible for a major difficulty with her poetry, the separation it effects between language and reality.

> The autogenerative concentration on language both reflects and was caused by Emily Dickinson's withdrawal from the world. She withdrew in all the physical ways with which we are familiar, and we must at long last consider what the effect was on her poems. Most crucially, her language

became idiosyncratic, disengaged from outside authority, and thus in its own way inimitably disordered. The lack of architecture is a consequence of the linguistic reflexiveness, and both are part of the harsh artistic freedom that opens up when reality and language undergo a separation. . . . When she disengaged her idiom from the complicated texture of social existence, she made it self-conscious, private, and momentary in its grasp.

Ultimately, Porter claims, "when language breeds, removed from exterior referents, it becomes almost pure locution, and meaning cannot be established."[4]

It is clear that behind the various "assessments" of Dickinson in these books are operating some very powerful assumptions about gender and art. If to be a fulfilled woman is to follow the model of Mrs. Dickinson, wife, mother (and invalid), to marry some Robert Browning, or at least somebody, then Dickinson's refusal to leave her father's house, her own bedroom, and her own mind is decidedly "unfeminine." At the very least, according to these writers, it leads to frustration and unhappiness. It may also lead to madness and to a severed connection with reality (probably these are the same). The mind, on the other hand, is masculine (according to Cody), and, according to both Whicher and Cody, so is poetry. Porter, on the other hand, makes a point of applauding Dickinson for being a woman poet, for understanding and writing about a woman's life, but he never looks to see any connections between the acts of her life, like the famous withdrawal, the acts of her poetry, such as its concern with mental experience, and her womanhood.

The mind may be thought of by some as "masculine," but men, even male poets, rarely *live* in the mind, as if it were, let us say, a house and they the householders there, the house*wives*. Although Dickinson's move into her mind is usually classified as "unfeminine," the way in which she made use of her mind is suspiciously "feminine." It's confusing, and worrisome, even when the poetry that was produced by all of this isn't. Because Dickinson is not a man, and is not a "real" woman, either, the complications that her situation creates for many critics results in either a radical schism in their thinking between "Dickinson the woman" and "Dickinson the poet" or in a total concentration on what resulted from all of this, her poems, with little or no acknowledgment that anybody at all wrote them.[5]

Of course, not all writing on Dickinson is so judgmental. Richard Sewall's eminently intelligent biography, *The Life of Emily Dickinson,* for example, begins by emphasizing "the degree to which her way of life represented a conscious choice. . . . More than is true of almost any other poet in the tradition, her life, like the major vehicle of her poetry, was metaphoric; and as she grew older, it became more and more deliberately so."[6] Sewall's portrait of Dickinson is sensitive to her traits and her techniques; it persists as an invaluable source of information about her. What it does not do is analyze the poetry, and it does not raise the question of gender—that is, look at how Dickinson's womanhood affects either her life choices, for example, the suggestive fact that her life was "metaphoric," or her poetry.

A concern with gender is central to feminist criticism, which characterizes Dickinson's move into the mind as strategy rather than retreat. Feminist criticism begins with the assumption that gender informs the nature of art, the nature of biography, and the relation between them. Dickinson is a woman poet, and this fact is seen as integral to her identity.

Recent studies of Dickinson from a feminist perspective, including Sandra M. Gilbert and Susan Gubar's *The Madwoman in the Attic: The Woman Writer and the Nineteenth-Century Literary Imagination,* Karl Keller's *The Only Kangaroo Among the Beauty: Emily Dickinson and America,* Margaret Homans's *Women Writers and Poetic Identity: Dorothy Wordsworth, Emily Brontë, and Emily Dickinson,* Joanne Feit Diehl's *Dickinson and the Romantic Imagination,* and Barbara Clarke Mossberg's *Emily Dickinson: When a Writer Is a Daughter* share a set of basic assumptions as they discuss various aspects of Dickinson's life and work.[7] First, they assume that Dickinson's actions make sense and that her actions and her poetry are related in a way that also makes sense as well as art. These writers do not separate woman from poet, and they assume that the woman poet can assert control over herself, her life, her work. Granting to Dickinson knowledge and responsibility for what she did, they try to interpret and understand her according to her own terms. They respect her own version of herself. Finally, they see in Dickinson not only control but power, power derived from creating a world in which she could be herself, from creating a self with which she could accomplish her best.

"Strategy" means that Dickinson chose to keep to her house, to her room, to live in her mind rather than in the external world, in order to achieve certain goals and to circumvent or overcome certain forces in her environment and experience that were in opposition to those goals—particularly, the expectations and norms that a patriarchal society creates for women, especially problematic when a woman wants to be a poet.

In my first study of women poets, *Naked and Fiery Forms: Modern American Poetry by Women, A New Tradition,* I use the phrase, "the double bind of the woman poet," to talk about the conflict and strain experienced by women poets in our society, because "woman" and "poet," as much traditional literary criticism indicates, denote opposite and contradictory qualities and roles.[8]

Dickinson's way of declaring her vocation, from her early letters to friends and to her brother to her famous dialogue with the editor, Thomas Wentworth Higginson, is a good example of the effects of the double bind. Dickinson cloaks her avowals in various metaphors; she attests at once to her bravery and her wickedness; she apologizes for herself; but through it all she keeps declaring herself to be a writer.

In 1850, when she is twenty, she characterizes her friend Abiah Root as a good, proper, "real" girl, making Abiah a foil for her own self-portrait as deviant.

> Now my dear friend, let me tell you that these last thoughts are fictions – vain imaginations to lead astray foolish young women. They are flowers of speech, they both *make,* and *tell* deliberate falsehoods, avoid them as the snake, and turn aside from the *Bottle* snake, and I dont *think* you will be harmed. Honestly tho', a snake bite is a serious matter, and there cant be too much said, or done about it. The big serpent bites the deepest, and we get so accustomed to its bites that we dont mind about them. "Verily I say unto you fear *him*." Wont you read some work upon snakes – I have a real anxiety for you! I love those little green ones that slide around by your shoes in the grass – and make it rustle with their elbows – they are rather my favorites on the whole, but I would'nt influence *you* for the world![9]

Margaret Homans has shown in convincing detail how Dickinson associates language, lies, sin—and portrays herself as Eve, sinner and poet—in this passage.[10] She is bad to Abiah's good, in every way; but how proudly she declares it: "I love those little green ones . . ."!

A similar irony and tension are manifest in another letter to Abiah from the same year.

> . . . You are growing wiser than I am, and nipping in the bud fancies which I let blossom – perchance to bear no fruit, or if plucked, I may find

it bitter. The shore is safer, Abiah, but I love to buffet the sea—I can
count the bitter wrecks here in these pleasant waters, and hear the mur-
muring winds, but oh, I love the danger! You are learning control and
firmness. Christ Jesus will love you more. I'm afraid he don't love me
any! . . .[11]

Most critics assume these "fancies" to be her plans to become a
poet. I agree, yet find it equally significant that she needs the veil of
allegory to say so, while at the very same time announcing her daring,
her sinfulness.

A letter to her brother Austin in 1853 shows her very much
aware of the male's prerogatives in the world of poetry yet also asserting her own claims, which turn out to be prior, and superior, to his.

> And Austin is a Poet, Austin writes a psalm. Out of the way, Pegasus,
> Olympus enough "to him," and just say to those "nine muses" that we
> have done with them!
>
> Raised a living muse ourselves, worth the whole nine of them. Up,
> off, tramp!
>
> Now Brother Pegasus, I'll tell you what it is—I've been in the habit
> *myself* of writing some few things, and it rather appears to me that you're
> getting away my patent, so you'd better be somewhat careful, or I'll call
> the police![12]

Ten years later, in her correspondence with Higginson, the constant humility that she adopts ("My size felt small—to me—I read your
Chapters in the Atlantic—and experienced honor for you—") is ac-
companied by statements that yet reveal her stubborn pride in herself
and sense of self-worth, although, as always, these unladylike assertions are masked: "If fame belonged to me, I could not escape her"; "I
do not let it go, [a line of poetry] because it is mine."[13]

From all of these examples it is clear that Dickinson knows full
well what a proper girl is and how one should behave; knows equally
well that her sense of her own self is profoundly deviant. Yet still she
persists in becoming herself, adopting strategies of language (her
truth told slant) that reveal the double bind she experiences as much
as they deal with it.

Language, of course, turns out to be Dickinson's greatest power
and best weapon. But in order to use it properly and most effectively
as a means of control and of creation, Dickinson needs to develop
strategies of living as well as writing.

John Cody is probably correct in observing that Dickinson found little in her mother to emulate, that she did indeed identify in rather powerful ways with her father and, especially, her brother. What is misleading is his evaluation of the situation as "abnormal." As a Freudian, Cody insists that a woman acquires female identity through positive identification with her mother. If this does not happen, he maintains, if she has suspicions "that to be a female is to be second-rate," if she cannot find another woman to act as a role model (though what is her fascination with the great English women writers—George Eliot, the Brontës, Elizabeth Barrett Browning—but that?), "she may at last be driven to pattern herself on a masculine model," which will lead to "an almost insurmountable crisis in sexual identity."[14]

But for Dickinson to feel that "to be a female is secondrate" was surely accurate, even as it was probably more "normal" than otherwise for her not to want to be like her mother, to see in her male relatives important qualities that she possessed as well, to seek to be like those few other women who did not tend to marry and to bear children and who were writers. Cody's gender definitions do, however, reflect those of Dickinson's society as well as his own, so that her so-called "crisis in sexual identity" would indicate, not her craziness, but the predictable result of her own personality coming into conflict with society's norms.

One way in which Dickinson attempted to deal with this situation was to try *not* to grow into a "woman." In their chapter on Dickinson, Sandra Gilbert and Susan Gubar have observed: "She must have decided that to begin with she could try to solve the problem of being a woman by refusing to admit that she was a woman."[15] The child persona who so persists in her poetry, her sometimes identification of herself with a boy, her refusal, after a certain time, to enter seriously into the courtship games of her social set—and then, of course, the notorious although, it must be emphasized, *gradual* withdrawal—all exemplify how she kept herself, on both psychic and social grounds, from ever having to enter into the arena of adult womanhood as her society decreed it to be.

In the same letter to Abiah Root from which I have quoted Dickinson's announcement of the fancies she is letting blossom and of how she loves to buffet the sea, she speaks as well of another friend, remarking: "She is more of a woman than I am, for I so love to be a child – Abby is holier than me – she does more good in her lifetime than I shall ever do in mine – she goes among the poor, she shuts the eye of the dying – she will be had in memorial when I am gone and forgotten."[16] Her identification with the child (she is twenty), because it is contrasted to what a "woman" does—good works, once again underlines her sense of herself as deviant, not young. The woman who goes among the poor would not be out buffeting the sea.

When Dickinson, in an oft-quoted letter to Susan Gilbert, talks at age twenty-two about marriage, in prose which is however an elaborate conceit, her preference for their virginal condition, her fear of the power of men, and her intense desire to maintain her own self-autonomy are all very much in evidence.

> How dull our lives must seem to the bride, and the plighted maiden, whose days are fed with gold, and who gathers pearls every evening; but to the *wife*, Susie, sometimes the *wife forgotten,* our lives perhaps seem dearer than all others in the world; you have seen flowers at morning, *satisfied* with the dew, and those same sweet flowers at noon with their heads bowed in anguish before the mighty sun; think you these thirsty blossoms will *now* need naught but – *dew*? No, they will cry for sunlight, and pine for the burning noon, tho' it scorches them, scathes them; they have got through with peace – they know that the man of noon, is *mightier* than the morning and their life is henceforth to him. Oh, Susie, it is dangerous, and it is all too dear, those simple trusting spirits, and the spirits mightier, which we cannot resist! It does so rend me, Susie, the thought of when it comes, that I tremble lest I, too, am yielded up.[17]

The particular images she uses for the sexual situation, of flowers, sun, noon, and dew, continue into her poems on these topics, as many commentators have observed, most notably Gilbert and Gubar in their Dickinson chapter, Joanne Dobson in her essay, " 'Oh, Susie, It Is Dangerous': Emily Dickinson and the Archetype of the Masculine," and Adalaide Morris in her essay, " 'The Love of Thee – A Prism Be': Men and Women in the Love Poetry of Emily Dickinson."[18] The strong irony in this particular passage does not convey ambivalence but astute social observation and a clear understanding of her own motivation. To perpetuate adolescence is a way to remain oneself, because sex, men, and the married condition all represent, here and in poems of Dickinson's that will be discussed later in this book, the loss of self. Gilbert and Gubar make the valuable association of Dickinson's ploys with Catherine Earnshaw in *Wuthering Heights,* whose own childhood remains in her adult consciousness as the time, and place, when she was herself. "For, like Catherine, as Dickinson grew into that inescapable sexual consciousness which her little girl pose postponed but did not evade, she realized she must move away from the androgynous freedom of childhood and began, therefore, to perceive the symbolic castration implicit in female powerlessness."[19]

Barbara Mossberg, in "Metaphysics of a Yankee Mother Goose: Emily Dickinson's 'Nursery Rhymes,'" points to Dickinson's persistent "saying 'no.'"

> If Dickinson does not feel she has much authority or power in her culture, she can at least say "no" to the demands her culture makes upon her and women in general. Thus we see Dickinson winning a freedom of sorts for herself by *not* joining sewing societies, music groups, or church groups, by *not* becoming "born again," by *not* getting married, by *not* leaving home. Saying "no" to a conventional life as a woman necessarily keeps Dickinson in a kind of childhood; childhood in this sense is not only a metaphor for confinement and repression, but also a retreat from the world's limiting expectations for women. "No" is for Dickinson "the wildest word we consign to Language" because it makes for possibility. Dickinson's child persona is in large measure a crucial aspect of her systematic refusal to become bound in a conventional woman's life.[20]

Nevertheless, Dickinson was attracted to people, men and women. Her friendships were never casual. Her letters as well as her poems, written to the friends of her girlhood, to male friends both identified and unidentified, to older women and younger nieces, all show how overwhelmingly significant those she loved were to her. Love itself was for her an essential, and consuming, emotion. She did not choose not to marry and bear children because she could not, or would not, love. Her choice seems to have had more to do with her greater need to maintain her self and also with the way in which she did experience love. Sewall comments on her friendships as follows: "All her life she demanded too much of people. Her early girlfriends could hardly keep up with her tumultuous letters or, like Sue, could not or would not take her into their lives as she wanted to be taken. They had other concerns. The young men, save for a few who had amusing or edifying intellectual exchanges with her, apparently shied away. Eliza Coleman's fear that her friends in Amherst 'wholly misinterpret' her, was a polite way of saying, perhaps, that they would not respond with the intensity she apparently demanded of everyone." Sewall continues: "meetings themselves became ordeals . . . in her own economy, she found that she had to ration them very carefully."[21]

Given her propensity for passions more intense than their recipients could return, Dickinson used physical distance, and language, to deal with love. "After you went," she wrote to her friend Mrs. Holland, "a low wind warbled through the house like a spacious bird, making it high but lonely. When you had gone the love came. I supposed it would. The supper of the heart is when the guest has gone."[22]

Thus, because of her own temperament, her intensity and sensitivity; because of her ambitions for herself, her stubborn dedication to her sense of vocation; because of her situation as a woman in middle-class Amherst society in nineteenth-century America with its expectations for normal womanhood; Emily Dickinson, a woman who wanted to be a poet, chose to withdraw from the external world and to live her most significant life in the world of her mind. This decision was surely what enabled her to be the poet that she became. It gave her control over her own experience: she could select, apportion, focus, examine, explore, satiate herself exactly as she wished and needed to do, such that poetry could result. In the outer world, this manner of control would have been impossible. It gave her, as well, the possibility for complete and thorough experience, for risk, intensity, range, and depth, that as a woman she could never have achieved in the world at large. She could not wander across the continent, like Walt Whitman; but she could move freely in the "undiscovered continent," the mind.

Such a description of mental experience assumes, categorically, that these events are real. Even as Dickinson wishes to think of the mind itself as actual space, so she is insistent throughout her poetry that mental experience is in no way less real than what happens in the world outside. When David Porter writes of Dickinson's poems, "There is no final reality, and the loss of that reality is a function of a language intent on saying itself and not on signifying a specific world," or, "Dickinson had no subject, least of all reality," he is using a definition of reality that is based upon what he calls "the things outside her window,"[23] one which does not include in its domain mental experience. This approach does a profound disservice to the poetry Dickinson did write, because its subject is so often exactly that: what happens in the mind.

What happens in the mind is also the subject of this book. It is common enough to hear, of Emily Dickinson's life, that "nothing happened to her." "Nothing," in fact, tends to happen to most women, because, as we know, patriarchal history has a propensity for cataloguing battles and not dinner parties. Feminist history has begun to write the events of women's lives and call them real—not only their battle to get the vote but their daily domestic occurrences. Yet Dickinson's most important life took place not when she was baking the family's bread, but when she was adventuring, dangerously and alone, in the very deep and very wide terrain of her mind: having experiences so profound and powerful that they could be the subject of great poetry. For Dickinson did not choose to be a "normal" woman, even as she did not try to pretend that she was a man. She did not choose to live where men live, in the public world, or where women live, in the domestic world. She found another place, at once more private and expansive than either of those others: the mind.

And yet I do not think that Dickinson was the first woman to discover the mind's potential as a place particularly suited for significant experience. As Patricia Meyer Spacks writes in her study of the female imagination, "The cliché that women, more consistently than men, turn inward for sustenance seems to mean, in practice, that women have richly defined the ways in which imagination creates possibility: possibility that society denies . . . women dominate their own experience by imagining it, giving it form, writing about it."[24]

To live in the mind, an actual and occupied place, was for Dickinson the key to solving the problem of how to be a poet, of how to achieve the self-knowledge, the self-awareness, the self-fulfillment that her vocation demanded. Certainly Dickinson's tactics were extreme; but then, they were more successful than moderation might have brought. She became an extraordinary poet, as few women before or since have done. Nevertheless, I think that Dickinson was capitalizing upon a technique that women have always known and used, for survival, using the imagination as a space in which to create some life other than their external situation. What Dickinson did was to make art from it.

Virginia Woolf's Mrs. Ramsay, that classic wife and mother, is no solitary at all but a woman whose life is almost entirely involved in, defined by, other people and her relationship to them. Yet Woolf depicts her seeking at moments another kind of experience, one occurring within herself, that bears remarkable resemblance to what Dickinson undertook on a much grander scale.

And that was what now she often felt the need of—to think; well, not even to think. To be silent; to be alone. All the being and the doing, expansive, glittering, vocal, evaporated; and one shrunk, with a sense of solemnity, to being oneself, a wedge-shaped core of darkness, something invisible to others. Although she continued to knit, and sat upright, it was thus that she felt herself; and this self having shed its attachments was free for the strangest adventures. When life sank down for a moment, the range of experience seemed limitless. . . . This core of darkness could go anywhere, for no one saw it. They could not stop it, she thought, exulting. There was freedom, there was peace, there was, most welcome of all, a summoning together, a resting on a platform of stability.[25]

Mrs. Ramsay's inner voyaging provides her with an autonomy, a self-centeredness, that is missing in her daily life; it is her way of replenishing the self she gives away so readily, good woman that she is, so completely, to other people. Dickinson, however, did not give her self away. She hoarded it, guarded it, focusing all of her intelligence and courage on developing it fully. Making of herself a paradigm for everything, she did not have to find herself with and through others. That is why, even as the closed space of her mind granted her control over experience, the open space of her mind granted her supreme experience.

Therefore I am claiming that Dickinson's move into the mind can best be understood as occasioned by her social and psychological situation as a woman who wanted to be a poet. I am not claiming that men—in particular, male poets—have not also taken mental experience seriously, especially male poets writing in the Romantic tradition. But in understanding Dickinson's relation to that tradition, it is necessary to stress two distinctions.

The first is that a woman writer's relation to any masculine tradition *begins* by being that of outsider, not insider. As Sandra Gilbert and Susan Gubar have shown for a woman writing in the nineteenth century:

> . . . she must confront precursors who are almost exclusively male, and therefore significantly different from her. Not only do these precursors incarnate patriarchal authority. . . , they attempt to enclose her in definitions of her person and her potential which, by reducing her to extreme stereotypes (angel, monster) drastically conflict with her own sense of her self—that is, of her subjectivity, her autonomy, her creativity. On the one hand, therefore, the woman writer's male precursors symbolize authority; on the other, despite their authority, they fail to define the ways in which she experiences her own identity as a writer.

More, the masculine authority with which they construct their literary personae, as well as the fierce power struggles in which they engage their efforts of self-creation, seem to the woman writer directly to contradict the terms of her own gender definition. Thus the "anxiety of influence" that a male poet experiences is felt by a female poet as an even more primary "anxiety of authorship"—a radical fear that she cannot create, that because she can never become a "precursor" the act of writing will isolate or destroy her.[26]

Gilbert and Gubar, using Harold Bloom's concept of "anxiety of influence" as reference, show the primary and radical differences that separate any woman writer from the ongoing literary traditions of her times, "simply" because of the fact of her gender.

Margaret Homans explains more specifically the relationship between the tradition of Romantic poetry and nineteenth century women who wanted to be poets.

In Romantic poetry the self and the imagination are primary. During and after the Romantic period it was difficult for women who aspired to become poets to share in this tradition, not for constitutional reasons but for reasons that women readers found within the literature itself. Where the masculine self dominates and internalizes otherness, that other is frequently identified as feminine, whether she is nature, the representation of a human woman, or some phantom of desire. Although this tradition culminates in Romantic poetry, it originates in the Bible, which directly and through Milton's transmission reinforces the Romantic reading of gender. To be for so long the other and the object made it difficult for nineteenth-century women to have their own subjectivity. To become a poet, given these conditions, required nothing less than battling a valued and loved literary tradition to forge a self out of the materials of otherness. It is not surprising that so few women succeeded at this effort; very few even conceived of the possibility of trying.[27]

Homans goes on to show how Dickinson capitalized on her sense of otherness—as Eve, as sinner, as liar—to create a language that could articulate her subjectivity. But in doing this Dickinson finds her strength in her estrangement from the tradition, not from identification with it.

Joanne Feit Diehl is adamant on this point: "The degree to which Dickinson risks all, her quality of radical experimentation, is, I would argue, intimately connected to her sense of herself as estranged from the tradition. Any theory of poetic influences must account for the sex of the poet, and the question of Dickinson's sense of estrangement from the tradition is fundamentally involved with her awareness of her own isolation, and the freedom and particular burdens such an exclusionary relation to the tradition permits.[28]

The Romantic tradition of poetry in nineteenth-century England and America, in its variations, is not beside the point; but what we are dealing with at all times in seeing Dickinson in relation to it is the initial fact of dislocation—and then the differences, the difficulties, and the strategies to which this relation gave rise.

The second point is surely one of those differences. Dickinson did more than "take mental experience seriously": she took the mind to be an actual place, in which to set up housekeeping. The extraordinary number of analogies to house and home that Dickinson uses to describe the mind itself, as Jean Mudge, and others, have pointed out,[29] indicates not only the spatial dimensions that Dickinson assigns to the mind but also the way in which she occupies it. For all that she is clear about the mind's vast and awesome dimensions, which make it equivalent to the wide world, the entire universe as a field for exploration, she is equally clear that the mind is like a house, like a room, which she keeps in order, as she has been trained to do. Surely her peculiar use of the mind as a place in which to dwell as well as a place of which to write was primary among the strategies with which she enabled herself to become a woman poet in the tradition of literary Romanticism in which poets of her time were writing.

Hence my concentration in this study of Dickinson's poetry upon her poems that describe mental experience. In this chapter I look at Dickinson's poems about the space of the mind: the undiscovered continent, the landscape of the spirit. Its characteristics as an environment shed light upon the activities taking place within its perimeters and also upon the woman who created this situation for herself. In describing the mind as a setting for significant experience, Dickinson's language is characterized by an elaborate spatial vocabulary. Specifically, terms drawn from architecture, geography, and space-travel define a location that is enclosed, private, yet changeable in dimension, that can alter suddenly and violently, that can become vast and limitless.

2

Dickinson's poems frequently assert her sense of the mind's actuality with images of caverns and corridors (777, 670), windows and doors (303, 657), even cellars (1182). Because she took the mind to be her dwelling place, it is appropriate that she use these domestic figurative correspondences to describe it. Yet her poems using such architectural analogues go beyond pointing out how a mind might be like a house. They set out to show, as well, what happens in a mind that is as a house, so that the solidity which door and window frame provide grants substance both to the setting and to the events occurring within. The architectural vocabulary usually portrays the mind as an enclosed space, its confinement responsible for power, safety, yet fearful confrontation.

Poem 303 is a strong statement about the power of the self alone. The soul is shown living within a space defined by door, gate, and mat. The external world, with its nations and their rulers, is kept outside.

> The Soul selects her own Society –
> Then – shuts the Door –
> To her divine Majority –
> Present no more –
>
> Unmoved – she notes the Chariots – pausing –
> At her low Gate –
> Unmoved – an Emperor be kneeling
> Upon her Mat –
>
> I've known her – from an ample nation –
> Choose One –
> Then – close the Valves of her attention –
> Like Stone –

Traditional ideas about power are reversed here. Not control over vast populations but the ability to construct a world for oneself comprises the greatest power, a god-like achievement, announces the opening stanza. Not only is the soul alone "divine," but it is also identified as "Society" and "Majority": the poem also challenges our ideas about what constitutes a social group. Consequently, the enclosed space of the soul's house is more than adequate for a queenly life, and ambassadors of the external world's glories, even emperors, can easily be scorned. Yet while the speaker claims her equality with those most powerful in the outer world—they may be emperors, but she is "divine Majority," at the same time she asserts her difference from them; for her domestic vocabulary of door, low gate, and mat establishes her dwelling as not a grand palace but rather a simple house.

While associating power with the enclosed space of the mind, the poem also implies how isolation is confinement, too. When the soul turns in upon her own concerns, she closes "the Valves of her attention – / Like Stone –."

Valves permit the flow of whatever they regulate in one direction only: here, from outside to inside. Either of the halves of a double door or any of the leaves of a folding door are valves. Valves seen as doors reinforce the poem's house imagery, while their association with stone makes the walls separating soul from world so solid as to be, perhaps, prison-like.

Prison-like because they allow no escape from the kinds of conflict, the kinds of terror, even, that must occur within. Poem 670, exaggerating the architectural vocabulary, compares the chambers of the mind to the haunted castle of gothic fiction, a stereotypical setting for horror.

> One need not be a Chamber – to be Haunted –
> One need not be a House –
> The Brain has Corridors – surpassing
> Material Place –
>
> Far safer, of a Midnight Meeting
> External Ghost
> Than its interior Confronting –
> That Cooler Host.
>
> Far safer, through an Abbey gallop,
> The Stones a'chase –
> Than Unarmed, one's a'self encounter –
> In lonesome Place –
>
> Ourself behind ourself, concealed –
> Should startle most –
> Assassin hid in our Apartment
> Be Horror's least.
>
> The Body – borrows a Revolver –
> He bolts the Door –
> O'erlooking a superior spectre –
> Or More –

The poem assumes that the mind is substantial, possessing corridors and chambers, because it is the dwelling place of "oneself." The extended comparison that is developed, between two kinds of dwellings, two kinds of hauntings, is for the purpose of dramatizing how there can be something more frightening than the most frightening situation usually imaginable.

Both the second and third stanzas begin with the same phrase: "Far safer." Safer are the supernatural events of gothic castles, meeting ghosts at midnight; we are warned about "interior confronting," the everyday moments of the mind, another lonesome place, when "one's a'self encounter." One clue to the degree of difference in horror is the word, "Unarmed." We come prepared to find ghosts in spooky old castles, but not in what Dickinson calls in another poem "That polar privacy / A soul admitted to itself" (1695).

There is, in fact, no way one can be armed against this particular kind of ghost. The murderer seeking to kill the body can be vanquished—one can borrow a revolver, bolt the door. But this assassin is hidden within oneself—is oneself. There is no escape. As Dickinson comments in poem 894, "Of Consciousness, her awful Mate / The Soul cannot be rid."

In the final stanza, the quintessence of this horror is revealed. The rhetoric of the poem has been dramatic as well as concrete. Two dramas, in fact, have been enacted and contrasted. The external self has been venturing into lonesome abbeys, discovering hidden assassins in her chamber, even as the internal self has become aware of the existence of the "Cooler Host." Now the two plots turn into one. The self, who is, after all, body and mind at once, bolts the door, only to discover that she has locked herself in with herself. Adventuring in the external world, one need not confront one's own consciousness. But when one turns from "Horror's least" to live in the mind, that "superior spectre" can never be avoided again.

Because consciousness is self-confrontation, it establishes a "society" within, of "ourself" with "ourself." To represent the conflict and struggle engendered here, poem 642 uses an architectural vocabulary that provides a setting, fortress, for a drama of siege and defense. Yet even as "One need not be a Chamber – to be Haunted –" constructs a comparison between external and internal ghost stories only to conflate them, so the following poem's distinctions between inner and outer, protagonist and antagonist, turn out to be fictions.

Me from Myself – to banish –
Had I Art –
Impregnable my Fortress
Unto All Heart –

But since Myself—assault Me—
How have I peace
Except by subjugating
Consciousness?

And since We're mutual Monarch
How this be
Except by Abdication—
Me—of Me?

[642]

The speaker of the poem "Myself" wishes for the ability to banish from her castle an enemy, called "Me." In the second stanza she admits to the complexity of the problem; more than skill is required to maintain the defense, because there is a profound connection between the combatants. Reversing their titles—"Me" is now the speaker, "Myself" the opponent—the poem acknowledges their interchangeability while at the same time continuing to deal with them as separate entities. The enemy is also identified as "Heart" in the first stanza, "Consciousness" in the second. That these are as much aspects of "Me" as they are of "Myself" the poem will not yet admit.

Although we know that the poem is discussing one person and not two, its dramatic fiction of attacker and attacked creates a situation that is surely war, albeit civil. When the dichotomy itself is collapsed in the final stanza, the effect is to intensify the situation, the pain, the impossibility of victory. "Mutual Monarch," the antagonists are revealed to be in actuality both within. There is nobody without. Without doesn't matter. Victory is impossible, is not a mere matter of "art," because enemy and friend are one. "Consciousness" is the self's awareness of itself and could be vanquished only through the annihilation of self, which would leave no victor, since no self is left. The very naming of the characters in this drama articulates and also anticipates this conclusion. If in stanza one the defender was Myself, the attacker, Me; and in stanza two the attacker was Myself, the defender, Me; in the final stanza they, as mutual Monarch, are "Me" and "Me."

The poem's structure dramatizes an experienced conflict. If the fictional dichotomy of within and without is necessary so that we might understand the problem, so is the final denial of the fiction, that we might better understand the conclusion: that self-consciousness means precisely the encounter of the self with itself, and that this is a perpetual struggle.

Another house of the mind shows us one further element in its haunting: memory. Although events finish, consciousness persists. Its knowledge continues to inform every present with the past, whether we like it or not.

> Remembrance has a Rear and a Front—
> 'Tis something like a House—
> It has a Garret also
> For Refuse and the Mouse.
>
> Beside, the deepest Cellar
> That ever Mason laid—
> Look to it by its Fathoms
> Ourselves be not pursued—
>
> [1182]

Memory, perceived as a house, has dimensions that attest to the nature of its power. If it has front and rear and a nice high attic, it also has a deep, deep cellar. Its ghost lives in the cellar, those depths where memory broods and takes root. Memory is the house, the inhabitant is "ourselves." Again, a fiction of container and contained is established only to be denied by the conclusion of the poem. The "Fathoms" that pursue us are our own memory, after all: self is haunted by self.

Yet, as this group of poems indicates, such confrontation is continually necessary that the self might develop its complete capacities. Also, the poems show how conflict in the enclosed space of the mind differs from what happens in the outer world. Here it may cause trouble—but not loss. Never do the components of consciousness leave one another. Death, if it should come, kills all of the "Me's."

In all of these poems the enclosure experienced in the place of the mind, an enclosure that can mean confinement and internal strife, is established with an architectural vocabulary. Yet those same windows and doors can as well outline the spaciousness that only the imagination can create, reminding us once again of the power that is derived from the cultivation of consciousness.

> I dwell in Possibility—
> A fairer House than Prose—
> More numerous of Windows—
> Superior—for Doors—
>
> Of Chambers as the Cedars—
> Impregnable of Eye—

And for an Everlasting Roof
The Gambrels of the Sky —

Of Visitors — the fairest —
For Occupation — This —
The spreading wide my narrow Hands
To gather Paradise —

[657]

At first glance this poem may appear not to be about the mind; because although the place where the speaker lives, Possibility, is definitely a house, its chambers are "as the Cedars," its roof "the Gambrels of the Sky." However, it would be wrong to assume that this house is the house of nature. Rather, the poem is explaining that the imagination can be as vast as the subjects of its speculations. The language building this house attests to its figurative construction. Its rooms are not cedars but like cedars—solid, "Impregnable of Eye." Its roof is as high as the sky. The sky has, literally, no gambrels; but if one were to imagine a roof-like sky, then that would be the room of this house.

This house is "Possibility," the imagination. Dwelling there, the lady of the manor makes not cakes but poetry. Possibility becomes associated with poetry in stanza one, when it is contrasted with its opposite—not impossibility, but prose. Thus, the occupation of she who lives in the mind, the spreading wide her narrow hands "to gather Paradise," may be interpreted as the creation of poetry. Paradise is the farthest space conceivable, and the mind can expand to include it. When this happens, because of the power of the imagination, the "housewife" can be a poet.

3

For the mind, conceived of spatially, has properties other than those of enclosure. Its area and circumference are not fixed but, rather, changeable in dimension. The mind can expand, can grow wider and wider, under the demands of experience. To depict her sense of this kind of development, Dickinson frequently uses not an architectural but a geographical vocabulary. In the following poem, the cause of change is not identified, but its effects are shown to be profound.

The Brain, within its Groove
Runs evenly – and true –
But let a Splinter swerve –
'Twere easier for You –

To put a Current back –
When Floods have slit the Hills –
And scooped a Turnpike for Themselves –
And trodden out the Mills –

[556]

Here the mind's sudden alteration is compared to a river that has flooded; once enlarged, neither can be returned to their original confines. Yet, with characteristic hyperbole, Dickinson asserts that the two events are similar but not equal: it would be *harder* to return the brain to its normal activity than to undertake an entirely herculean feat in nature. Natural acts serve as comparisons for mental events in these poems of geographical vocabulary, but what happens in the mind is always more significant, more interesting, and different.

In poem 928 a similar vocabulary of river and flood describes the mind in a state of expansion.

The Heart has narrow Banks
It measures like the Sea
In mighty – unremitting Bass
And Blue Monotony

Till Hurricane bisect
And as itself discerns
Its insufficient Area
The Heart convulsive learns

That Calm is but a Wall
Of unattempted Gauze
An instant's Push demolishes
A Questioning – dissolves.

[928]

The first stanza equates the heart in its ordinary everyday placidity to the sea. Its perimeters are confined, its beat regular. Into this landscape crisis comes as hurricane to "bisect" the heart, now "convulsive." As the measurements of the heart are violently altered, the self learns that it has been contained by the thinnest and most easily rent of walls.

The poem shows how readily the dimensions of the mind can be changed. And, for all the danger involved when this happens, there is a corresponding excitement. The poem has described the heart on an ordinary day as mighty but also dull in its "Blue Monotony." Also, there is more wrong here than sheer boredom. In stanza three its narrow banks are equated with calm, described as a wall of "unattempted Gauze": the heart is so placid because nothing has ever happened to it. This is the quiescence of ignorance. Anything that smacks of significant experience, "an instant's Push," a "Questioning," is going to rupture that kind of wall. The heart is going to grow. Not slowly or organically but suddenly, violently: "convulsive." Once its insufficient area has expanded, it is not going to return to its original condition again.

The subsequent situation—what happens after this change occurs—is addressed by other poems that also use geographical metaphor.

> The inundation of the Spring
> Enlarges every soul—
> It sweeps the tenement away
> But leaves the Water whole—
>
> In which the soul at first estranged—
> Seeks faintly for its shore
> But acclimated—pines no more
> For that Peninsula—
>
> [1425]

Here the change is seen as salutary rather than fearful, spring as opposed to hurricane. But its form is the same, heavy weather, and so is its effect: an enlargement that dislocates careful boundaries which serve also as supports. The soul, land-locked at the outset, by the poem's end has become a sea creature. The soul can get used to being bigger; although the state is dangerous, it has its benefits. In fact, others of Dickinson's poems that I will study subsequently show the sea to be a persistent representation of consciousness at its most expanded, which is eternity.

Experience is the change that alters the mind's boundaries. Although this means trauma, it leads to insight, as poem 419 explains.

> We grow accustomed to the Dark—
> When Light is put away—

As when the Neighbor holds the Lamp
To witness her Goodbye –

A Moment – We uncertain step
For newness of the night –
Then – fit our Vision to the Dark –
And meet the Road – erect –

And so of larger – Darknesses –
Those Evenings of the Brain –
When not a Moon disclose a sign –
Or Star – come out – within –

The Bravest – grope a little –
And sometimes hit a Tree
Directly in the Forehead –
But as they learn to see –

Either the Darkness alters –
Or something in the sight
Adjusts itself to Midnight –
And Life steps almost straight.

As in 670, "One need not be a Chamber – to be Haunted," an event in the external world is contrasted, by means of the same vocabulary, with an event in the mind; their similarities underline their differences—in significance, in location.

The homely scene of the opening two stanzas, where a visitor leaving the lamplight of a friendly room and venturing into the night is at first shaken by the sudden darkness and then grows used to it, is symbolic of what happens whenever comfort and security are removed, when the unknown takes their place. We adjust, says the poem, as vision does.

"And so," begins the analogy in stanza three, "of larger – Darknesses – / Those Evenings of the Brain." Since the mind is a place, it, too, has evenings, and darknesses. Larger darknesses, however, because they are not merely a matter of lunar cycles, external in nature, but are psychic and spiritual, are far more encompassing in their extent and effect. This darkness is like the hurricane of 923 or the inundation of the spring in 1425, that major change which causes a corresponding reaction from the self. The action is dangerous; one can get hurt in the process, hit a tree. Nevertheless, adjustment occurs: under significant pressure the soul enlarges, even as, in the presence of darkness, the pupil of the eye will expand in order to see.

At the same time, the darkness itself can also alter, changing in response to the reaction of the particular self as it experiences this particular darkness. Here Dickinson hints at the complexity of the process that she is describing. Whereas "The Heart has narrow Banks" or "The inundation of the Spring" show external events to be opaque, fixed, while the self is responsive, changeable, now she indicates that the process can be reciprocal. The mind can equally alter events, for sight is, after all, not a one-way operation.

"Life steps almost straight," concludes the poem. Sight brings insight, all of these poems make clear. The experience will more likely than not be painful; the change in the mind's shape will hurt. Dickinson's descriptions of variations in area and circumference of mental space dramatize this situation. Thus many poems expand mental space from the confines of one "house." A geographical vocabulary articulates such expansion.

When the geographical vocabulary is also political, Dickinson returns to the issue of power, struggle or unity within the territory of the self, that concerned her in poems like "Me from Myself – to banish" (642).

> The Heart is the Capitol of the Mind –
> The Mind is a single State –
> The Heart and the Mind together make
> A single Continent –
>
> One – is the Population –
> Numerous enough –
> This ecstatic Nation
> Seek – it is Yourself.
>   [1354]

In "Me from Myself – to banish" Dickinson's political metaphor described a condition of division within the self; here, it helps her to explain an equally true sense of unity. In the kingdom of the self she grants reigning authority to feeling (Heart) but maintains at the same time that it is emotion plus intellect, Heart plus Mind, in interrelation, that forms one impressively large entity, a continent. Heart and Mind, occupying different areas in the body, serve to delineate the boundaries of the kingdom. Taken together, they define the self, who lives in that body. The political vocabulary shows how the different parts of a whole work together to make it one. We know from other poems that this situation may be a truce instead of a treaty, yet the state as she reveals it here is as genuine as the horror she also experiences.

The poem continues, like "The Soul Selects her own Society" (303) or "I dwell in Possibility" (657), to praise the standard of living in such a kingdom where the population of one is "Numerous enough." Certainly Dickinson finds in exploring that "Single Continent" a varied number of climates and terrains, all of which are herself, even as she is all of its inhabitants. By thus boldly graphing with a geographical vocabulary the contours of a world, by populating it with a complete society that is one self, Dickinson describes the richness of the mental life.

4

But the dimensions of the mind can be vaster yet. There is another vocabulary for talking about the brain, not merely spatial but outer-spatial. There are ways in which the mind can be as immense as the universe. Some of her poems describe extraterrestrial travel.

> I stepped from Plank to Plank
> A slow and cautious way
> The Stars about my Head I felt
> About my Feet the Sea.
>
> I knew not but the next
> Would be my final inch –
> This gave me that precarious Gait
> Some call Experience.
>
> > [875]

This extraordinary vision of herself with stars about her head, with the sea at her feet is meant to be true, but it is not occurring in external space. It occurs where visions usually do, in the mind. Internal space is the setting for this adventure, and the poem specifically identifies the exploration that has brought her there as the quest for experience. She has become enormous, tall as the universe, equivalent to the universe. The precariousness of her enterprise, its danger as well as achievement, is responsible for her magnitude.

Poem 378, another expedition into space, calls attention to the mind's fluid structure. Enclosure and expansion are at issue in an extreme form.

> I saw no Way – The Heavens were stitched –
> I felt the Columns close –

The Earth reversed her Hemispheres –
I touched the Universe –

And back it slid – and I alone –
A Speck upon a Ball –
Went out upon Circumference –
Beyond the Dip of Bell –

As the poem begins, its speaker is experiencing the total constriction that we remember from the conclusion to 303, when the "Valves of her attention" close, "like Stone." Here, too, the columns close, and an image of near-suffocation (a domestic metaphor, of sewing, put to murderous purpose) intensifies the situation: "The Heavens were stitched." The explorer is stymied, until suddenly the brain's propensity for widening, for opening out, is enacted. The closed circle that traps her turns inside out. First she touches the universe; then that, too—one limit or edge of knowledge, of experience, of consciousness, is removed, and she is further out still, where nothing of the known world is left. She is at the edge of everything, of anything, "out upon Circumference." Circumference, "the farthest boundary of human experience,"[30] is a significantly spatial term, emphasizing dimension. Outer space is equivalent to the extent and the limits of knowing; hence its existence within as well as without the mind. The outer-spatial vocabulary, here as in other such poems, with its dramatic exaggerations, grants to the mind a vastness of width, depth, and height that is the other side of those poems of architectural vocabulary, which outline the enclosed space of the mind.

Dickinson's poems that describe the mind, using vocabularies from architecture, geography, and space travel, assert both the actuality of the mind and also its supremacy. By conceiving of the mind as a world, by conceiving of the exploration of the mind as ultimate experience, she provides both a rationale and an apologia for her chosen lifestyle. To live in the mind is to be most thoroughly alive, these poems indicate. Poem 632 explains why this can be.

The Brain – is wider than the Sky –
For – put them side by side –
The one the other will contain
With ease – and You – beside –

The Brain is deeper than the sea –
For – hold them – Blue to Blue –
The one the other will absorb –
As Sponges – Buckets – do –

The Brain is just the weight of God –
For – Heft them – Pound for Pound –
And they will differ – if they do –
As Syllable from Sound –

This poem attests to the mind's supremacy over everything in the external world, to its easy equivalence with God. The actuality of the mind or brain, as there as sky or sea, is revealed through a vocabulary of dimension and measurement, of capacity and color. But though brain and world have this in common, there is a difference too: the brain is wider than the sky (widest thing in nature), deeper than the sea (deepest thing in nature). How can this be? The third stanza explains by comparing the brain to God Himself. Since God is the force that conceived of and created nature, He must be wider and deeper than anything in nature. Nature is only a part of God, who, in fact, functions like a brain. God and the brain both create by thinking. Dickinson finds her brain and God to be equivalent: their possible difference being that of "Syllable from Sound," or the difference between undifferentiated power and language as a specific form of that power—poetic creation as opposed to cosmic creation. Like God, the mind is, and is greater than, whatever it thinks about; because it contains what it thinks about, and more: the ability to think about. Consequently, if the poet wishes for total experience, if she is daring and dedicated enough to pursue this quest, she can do no better than to explore, then write about, the place of the mind.

That place, enclosed and private, can provide protection, safety, sanctity: yet it demands as well the struggle of self-consciousness. If there is no easy entrance here, there is also no easy exit. Yet the mind is fluid in form, changeable in dimension. Profound experience can alter its shape and size, suddenly, violently. If the self's encounter with the self is one major kind of trauma, another is this abrupt and painful change that must occur if there is to be significant experience and the insight that is produces. Insight is change in the very boundaries which circumscribe and define the mind's space. So that this space is also as vast as the outer space surrounding our world. Journeying towards the farthest reaches of consciousness brings one to the limits of knowing, where one may become most fully alive. In this way Dickinson sets out to discover the undiscovered continent, the mind: the place in which she lives.

ii *"To Make a Prairie"*

1

IN THE POEMS THAT define what happens in mental spaces—emotional and intellectual experience—Dickinson uses a poetic language and a formal structure that may be viewed as responses to the epistemological problems set by her subject matter. Vocabulary, figures of speech, structures of thought and stanza, modes of presentation—all contribute to the language that Dickinson fashions in order to talk about life in the mind. This chapter closely examines such language patterns, because they are the components that fit together to make the poems, and because in their own right they embody the philosophical issues raised by Dickinson when she explores the nature of mental experience. The relation between the world of the mind and the world of nature, between idea and object, are in question.

Dickinson's poetic vocabulary contains two special categories of words: dimensional—words of space and time—and conceptual—abstractions, the words for ideas. I have already discussed how spatial metaphors are necessary to describe the mind itself when it is conceived of as a place. Equally, acts occurring within the mind are rendered with a vocabulary that ascribes to them spatial and temporal dimensions. At the same time, and usually in the same poem, a conceptual vocabulary is present to establish the intellectual, theoretical aspects of the mind: the fact that it categorizes, generalizes, and hypothesizes on the basis of its own experience. Dickinson's poems reveal a structure based upon the encounter, dramatic and reciprocal, between the dimensional and conceptual vocabularies. This encounter is most frequently achieved with metaphors initiated by analogy.[1] In smaller and larger units—of phrase, line, sentence, stanza—analogy compares and conjoins abstract and concrete, idea and thing, the world of the mind and the world of nature. Analogy solicits the participation of nature for these representations of the mind's doings, if only because the natural world offers the poet available terminology for the concrete. Dickinson, after all, thinks of mental acts as real and is faced with the lack of an adequate language for expressing this attitude. Medical or even psychological terms, even if she had known them or if they had been invented, wouldn't do. She doesn't think of the brain as a muscle but as a place; she doesn't think of emotion as a symptom, but as an act. The life of the mind, although different in significant ways, bears a genuine relation to the life of the outer world. Therefore, nature is a frequent guest in Dickinson's poems about the mind, entering them via analogies that are constructed along an abstract-concrete axis.

The form of analogy is based upon parallelism. *A* is like *b; a* is *b;* or as *a*, so *b*—these are versions of the fundamental analogical pattern. Larger units—sentence, stanza, and argument—are often generated from this central structure. ("I call Dickinson an analogical poet," writes Robert Weisbuch, "because analogy suggests an extended equation [*a* is to *b* as *c* is to *d*] carried out by a rigorous logic whose comparisons are always functional and never decorative. Further, we may think of metaphor as a completed analogy, in which the progressive logic of the associations is buried; conversely, we may think of analogy as a metaphor-in-the-making, in which the associative process calls attention to itself."[2]) But because there are at the same time profound ways in which nature and the mind are as different as they are like, the parallelism that analogy encourages is rarely pure or neat in these poems. It is as much a rule to be broken as it is a ruler for poetic organization, so that formal development is frequently complicated by inversions, conversions, and other maneuvers in which parallelism is "exploded."

Finally, these analogical metaphors composed from dimensional and conceptual vocabularies that extend throughout the poem in parallel units are frequently presented as aphorisms: short, pithy statements avowing a general doctrine or truth. Dickinson may be describing personal, private experience (she was neither doctor nor psychologist, and her only subject was herself), yet she persistently categorizes it as everyone's. She speaks in general truths, and this is one reason why the conceptual vocabulary is as essential to her as the dimensional one. With its abstractions she defines and classifies experience; she establishes norms for behavior. The poems that thus diagram mental events are prescriptive as well as descriptive. Because of the striking generality of their rhetoric, they seem like blueprints: if you repeat the variables, you get the same experience, they suggest. In fact, one of the remarkable aspects of these poems, which is underlined by their aphoristic stance, is how, confined as they are to the dimensions of one mind, they so often speak for so many.

"Presentiment – is that long Shadow – on the Lawn –" (764); "Experience is the Angled Road" (910); "A still – Volcano – Life –" (601); "The Suburbs of a Secret" (1245); "Delight's Despair at setting" (1299); "My Faith is larger than the Hills –" (766): thus poems begin.

In each of these examples an abstraction—presentiment, experience, life, secret, delight, despair, faith—is connected by the process of metaphor to a concrete image—lawn, road, volcano, suburbs, hills. The connection is made in varying grammatical ways: through the verb, either the equation of the copula or the less direct but more active predication of *setting;* through nouns in apposition, *volcano, life;* through the possessive of preposition, explicit or implied, *suburbs* and *secret, delight* and *despair;* through the comparative adjective, *larger.* Whatever the form of transaction, in most cases the relation created between abstract and concrete calls attention to either the spatial or temporal qualities of the concrete ("larger than the Hills"; "long Shadow – on the Lawn"), so that these dimensions are transferred in some manner to the abstract word. Cristanne Miller points out that "the contrast of concrete and abstract diction makes the poet's images more immediate because the concrete aspect generally involves a sensual or commonly active response." Already in these first lines analogy is underway. As Miller notes, "Any predication of an abstract onto a concrete or concrete onto an abstract quality is necessarily metaphorical and therefore by definition refers directly to no established thing or relationship."[3] Also, the aphoristic voice is immediately present. As I proceed, I shall try to isolate these linguistic features as much as possible for the sake of clarifying the function and the significance of each, but it is obvious from this little catalogue of opening lines how very much a part of one another they really are. Vocabulary, figure, structure, tone—these are different perspectives on the same language.

Let us look at the continuation of one of these phrases to see what happens to its elements as they combine to make a poem.

> Presentiment – is that long Shadow – on the Lawn –
> Indicative that Suns go down –
>
> The Notice to the startled Grass
> That Darkness – is about to pass –

[764]

A mental state, presentiment, the feeling that something will happen, is equated with a shadow on the lawn. As the poem continues, the nature of the shadow is revealed. It is seen, in the second line, to function as a sign, coming before the fact of sunset. In the middle of one situation, afternoon, nature has ways of revealing the situation that is to follow. The metaphor begins by connecting the general emotion, presentiment, to a specific shadow; but by the sentence's conclusion the shadow is becoming itself generic, indicative not that the sun on this day but that suns in general set. The message has become prescriptive, aphoristic: a teaching text.

The second stanza appears to parallel the first; in apposition to the phrase, "Presentiment is," it offers another analogy. The scene is still the lawn. Both lines one and three end with it, even as the announcements of change that conclude lines two and four are also parallel: "go down"; "about to pass." But there are differences. In line three the concrete shadow of line one has turned into another abstraction, "the Notice." And the lawn has been personified: "startled." It is the mind that grants abstract meaning to the shadow, even as it understands the grass to have human emotions. If nature is akin to the mind, this is at least in part due to the fact that the mind interprets nature as well as itself. There are other ways, too, in which the parallelism of the second stanza has been altered, "exploded." The scene in nature is the same but different: the same lawn but a different shadow, the one that comes at dawn to announce not the setting but the rising of the sun. Dickinson's brief poem includes therefore the full cycle of nature: the onset of dark when it is still light, the onset of light when the dark is still there.

What does this have to do with presentiment? Presentiment is the apprehension of a signal for change. It is knowing ahead of time, yet it happens because change is inherent in a given condition. Presentiment is based on real, not hypothetical, evidence. Yet the sign, when it comes, comes as a shock. We may understand change as an abstract principle, but we have a habit of getting used to the way things are. Thus presentiment is a useful sensitivity, because, in offering foreknowledge, it stirs us from our sluggish, accepting ways and helps us get a jump on the forces of life. Presentiment occurs in nature, as it occurs in the mind. But of course, only a mind observing natural acts can understand them to be versions of presentiment.

As my discussion of the nature of presentiment in the previous paragraph indicates, all about us, not about her, the poem is a tidy aphorism, a statement of general truth. When Dickinson defines presentiment as that long shadow on the grass, she is calling it everybody's experience. She does this by labelling her personal feeling of something about to happen with a generic abstraction: presentiment. She does this by using the copula, *is:* not *can be* or *may be* or *in this case,* but confidently and radically, *is.* She does this by equating her feeling with an act in nature, one that, we understand as we read on into the poem, is governed by natural laws. Such rhetorical devices turn an individual perception into a truism.

Aphorism, in its compression and its comprehensiveness, is a hyperbolic mode. Some functions of Dickinson's dimensional and conceptual vocabularies are clarified when we observe their operation in aphorism. For example, the usefulness of words of dimension drawn from nature for the task of generalizing becomes apparent. Since natural laws are accepted as universal, Dickinson calls upon their validity to underwrite via analogy pronouncements about mental activity, less accessible for generalization because it is private rather than public.

Abstractions are her other means of generalizing. The fact that Dickinson's poems seeking to understand the workings of the mind are filled with abstractions indicates how the process of abstracting itself is an essential one in mental activity. Aphorism may sound like a generalization for everybody, but it is based on the mind's tendency to make rules for itself. "A finger in the flame brings pain," it says. Or, "Pain is the kiss of finger and flame." If you take one instance of putting a hand too near the fire and another instance of the same phenomenon, the mind will want to stop calling it "finger plus flame" and label it "pain." So that although Dickinson's poems use a single mind as subject rather than conducting experiments on others, they articulate, in an exaggerated rhetorical form, aphorism, a characteristic of their subject matter, the mind.

Yet the aphoristic form is hyperbolic, and Dickinson might have generalized upon the premises just discussed without pushing them so hard. There are several reasons why aphorism might have come readily to her. Her reading in the Bible, for example, her thorough grounding in a Christian way of handling and articulating experience, are certainly possible explanations. Karl Keller connects her use of aphorism with Emerson. She picked up the Emerson method, he argues, while "escaping the Emerson morality," so that "the Emerson sentence . . . became for her a hold on the universe."[4]

> Emerson gave Emily Dickinson a *way* to believe: her sententiousness is evidence of that. In the range of forms from the gnomic and aphoristic to the epigram and maxim, she found a security, perhaps something close to the illusion of fulfillment and permanence, even as she wanders . . . amid uncertainties, lost. . . . In the aphoristic, she plays at creating assurances for herself, determined to make her own enduring paradise. Considering her experiences to the point of generalization, like Emerson's Montaigne, she could maintain a strong ego and at the same time explore, however illusorily, what Emerson called "an unused universe."[5]

Keller connects this idea about the apparent stability of aphorism as concept with its function in the structure of her language:

> I would like to suggest in addition that the more formal syntax of this aphoristic style served Emily Dickinson as a corrective to the improvisations of her lines—that is, the erratic metaphors, the collapsed syntax, the roughened off-rhymes and off-rhythms, and the short-circuited ellipses, or what Louise Bogan argues is the style of a cat trying to speak English. Against this, Emily Dickinson is ordering the universe. Sententiousness, like the hymn meter played over against her own voice, is a location, a place, a space, a monument. In her aphoristic statements she replaces *I* with universals for the sake of balance—even though her personality never entirely disappears amid all the abstracting of possible truths.[6]

For Keller's "permanence" I would substitute "authority" and connect the odd combination of personalism and generalism represented by Dickinson's use of aphorism with her situation as a woman writer.

The rhetorical stance of aphorism, with both its bravado and reticence, is a verbal form equivalent to her overall presentation of self to world. Bravado, because the aphorisms claim such total and unequivocal knowledge. Reticence, because they never do reveal their personal basis. They make the private public without anybody knowing it, while at the same time they obliquely grant complete authority to the personal. They protect even as they project. (Dickinson's letters are so embedded with aphorisms, usually without the context that a poem provides with its one or several analogies, that they sometimes seem to be written in code. Sharon Cameron, commenting upon their protective function, remarks: "In Dickinson's letters we can observe that the more vested the relationship with the letter recipient, the more aphoristic, epigrammatic, and explicitly literary the letters become. . . ."[7])

The aphorisms represent a solution to the problem of authority that the woman writer has always faced. Since she is by definition not "man," since her experience, if she does not falsify it by trying to fit it into his, is therefore not "universal," how can she claim to have anything important to say? The woman writer's awareness of her traditional dilemma is evident in the way that Jane Austen apologizes (or does she?) for "the little bit (two Inches wide) of Ivory on which I work with so fine a Brush, as produce little effect after much labour";[8] the way that Anne Bradstreet, likewise apologizing (with a certain discernible irony) for her "foolish, broken, blemished Muse," begins her poem, "The Prologue":

> To sing of captains, and of kings,
> Of cities founded, commonwealths begun,
> For my mean pen are too superior things.[9]

"But simple I according to my skill," she concludes. In these remarks is evident a stance towards the problem that is like Dickinson's, albeit Dickinson's is, as everything else about her, exaggerated. (Marianne Moore in our own century uses aphorisms in a similar way, for, we might assume, similar reasons.) Austen and Bradstreet proclaim their inability to write as men do. This appears in the form of apology, but it turns out to be bravado, since they are at the same time claiming an ability to do something else and subtly disparaging the male mode in the bargain. The brush is fine, asserts Austen; the skill is there, asserts Bradstreet. Their novels and poems, situated in life experiences which are not those of captains and kings, bear witness to their ability.

The aphorisms that occur everywhere in Dickinson's poetry are linguistically equivalent to her lifestyle as I have described it earlier, where what looks like demurral, reticence, and self-abnegation can also be interpreted as a stubborn assertion of self-importance. Although the aphorisms by their very form take this stance, there are several of her poems in which stance itself is the theme.

> Good to hide, and hear 'em hunt!
> Better, to be found,
> If one care to, that is,
> The Fox fits the Hound —
>
> Good to know, and not tell,
> Best, to know and tell,
> Can one find the rare Ear
> Not too dull —
>
> [842]

In a poem where movement depends upon parallel structure, the speaker relates hiding, seeking, and finding to knowing, then telling—a process I will interpret as that of poetry. The central message here is that the fox and the poet hide not only out of a desire for privacy but out of an interest in the game itself; out of a desire to test the hound and the audience, a wish to be found only by the appropriate seeker. In each stanza there is a progression of explanations that are not contradictory but hierarchical. The stanzas are paralleled, and we can consider them to be versions of the same theme: the fox and hound story an analogy for the mental drama, and vice versa.

In the first stanza the speaker begins with a rather smug assessment of her situation, a pleasure derived from being hidden while everyone else has to look for you. This is equivalent, she says in stanza two, to knowing and not telling. It is an attitude of bravado, not at all that of the shy, shrinking violet. And yet, stanza one continues, it is after all "better" to be found than to be perpetually holding out; in fact, as the second line of stanza two asserts, it is "best" to tell what one knows. But there is a condition set upon coming out, telling. The finder must be able to search out this crafty hider; if he or she is up to the task, then and only then is publicity, or publication, worthwhile. The hound has to be as clever as the fox, as the listener or reader must be as intelligent as the poetry. Such a person is rare, she says; so that the coming out and the telling is, we assume, likewise rare. And of course, as line three of the first stanza remarks, one is only found if one cares to be. The essential superiority and power of the position taken by this fox is very clear.

One remains hidden, for the most part. But this hiding, as the poem demonstrates, is part of the process of being found and not an end in itself. Thus the being found or the telling might take of necessity subtle forms. In thinking about forms of telling, we should remember one of Dickinson's most well-known lines, surely relevant here: "Tell all the Truth but tell it slant – / Success in Circuit lies" (1129).

This need to protect and reveal, everywhere in Dickinson's life and work, is a way, as I discussed in chapter 1, of dealing with the "double bind" of the woman poet. Poetry is both a male and a public mode. Even as Dickinson needs to exaggerate the privateness of her "woman's" life, so she exaggerates, with aphorism, the publicness of poetry. The voice that speaks the aphoristic poems has often been called that of bard or seer: the most public of a poet's voices. Aphorism is for Dickinson a rhetorical technique that can at once claim enormous power for the personal and at the same time protect it.

2

In poems defining mental experience, language features such as vocabularies of dimension and concept, metaphors based in analogy, parallelism, and aphorism combine. Yet the nature of this combination is rarely simple, because the subject matter is entirely complex. The formal neatness of analogy and parallelism is useful because contrast clarifies. But in building poetic structures out of analogy and parallelism Dickinson makes combinations characterized by the intricacy of their arrangement. The following poem demonstrates the complexity that analogy and parallelism so often achieve.

The difference between Despair
And Fear – is like the One
Between the instant of a Wreck –
And when the Wreck has been –

The Mind is smooth – no Motion –
Contented as the Eye

Upon the Forehead of a Bust –
That knows – it cannot see –

[305]

The poem begins with an analogy comparing the difference between two emotional states possessing, we are to assume, aspects in common—despair and fear—to an example drawn from the world of nature: the difference between a wreck taking place and afterwards. A familiar inner-outer maneuver, except that the speaker's matter-of-fact tone of explanation (the difference between *a* and *b* is like that between *c* and *d*) is belied by the opaqueness of her terms. The difference between *c* and *d* is about as non self-evident as that between *a* and *b!* We look gratefully to the next stanza with its ostensible parallel structure for help.

Smooth; no motion: it appears to have been a shipwreck. Yet this new information in a concrete vocabulary does not describe the wreck after all, but the mind. The poem, setting out to explain an emotional state in terms of a physical state, doubles back on itself by further describing the physical state in terms of the mental state. Smooth and without motion, the mind feels like, not the instant of a wreck but when the wreck has been.

Next, smoothness and motionlessness are compared to a mental state, contentment (abstract explaining concrete). The mind is contented as an eye, a blind eye, one that knows it cannot see. But this eye is not an instance of synecdoche, because it is not the eye of the person whose mind this is all about but the stone eye of a statue. Such an eye would be smooth and motionless, but its "contentment" would be a negative virtue: the cessation of struggle in the face, as it were, of impossibility ("That knows – it cannot see").

By its conclusion the poem has presented three analogues for the difference between despair and fear, what Weisbuch calls "analogical progression" or "the analogical collection": "Each is at least partially analogous to the others and each reveals a new aspect or consequence of putting the world together in the particular, often unstated way which links the otherwise disparate examples," he explains.[10] Here the first analogue is the difference between the instant of a wreck and when the wreck has been; the second, the bridging analogy, describes the mind in one of these states, either despair or fear, the poem doesn't say, as like the moment when the wreck has been; the third is the comparison of this same state to the eye on a statue. The accumulation of analogies is supposed to result in our understanding of the two states of mind and of their relationship. Any of the analogies alone won't do it: we need the combination.

The difference between the instant of a wreck and afterwards is that between struggle and its absence. The smooth surface after the ship has gone down is like the stone blind eye of the statue, with its power to do anything about its condition gone. The necessary content occasioned by this condition is as well a profound despair: the power-lessness to affect events. Fear comes during the instant of a wreck, despair afterwards. Fear is an active condition, despair passive: smooth, motionless, "content."

If we accept these definitions of despair and fear, we must invert the overt parallelism of the first analogy, which would be that despair is to the instant of a wreck as fear is to when the wreck has been. Such an inversion would consequently "explode" the parallelism. Yet that explosion of parallelism as well as the combination of analogues is exactly what tends to happen in these poems defining mental events. The complexity that they require is achieved, here as in "presen-timent – is that long Shadow – on the Lawn –," by changing the prede-termined route of parallelism when necessary. The very sense of shock that comes to the reader whenever this happens seems to be a part of the poem's purpose when it shows us how likeness, especially that between the world of the mind and the world of nature, at once exists and does not exist.

In other words, although analogy is possible between mind and nature—helpful and apt—there are real differences between these two places. Mental events and natural events are not at all mirror images of one another.

> "Nature" is what we see –
> The Hill – the Afternoon –
> Squirrel – Eclipse – the Bumble bee –
> Nay – Nature is Heaven –
> Nature is what we hear –
> The Bobolink – the Sea –
> Thunder – the Cricket –
> Nay – Nature is Harmony –
> Nature is what we know –
> Yet have no art to say –
> So impotent Our Wisdom is
> To her Simplicity.
>
>   [668]

In defining nature this poem both uses the poetic format that we have been discussing—the analogies, parallelism, aphorisms, concrete and abstract vocabularies are all here—and makes them its theme.[11]

The poem is a dialogue, or perhaps a trio, in which concrete and abstract, object and interpretation, are contrasted. The first voice begins. "Nature," it says, is apprehended with our senses; we see hill, afternoon, squirrel, eclipse, bumblebee. Nature is out there. No, corrects a second voice: nature is heaven. Heaven as a place may be created from the things, the objects that we see around us, but the arrangement is the mind's work.

These first four lines, in which point and counterpoint are sounded, are parallelled with four more lines that follow the same pattern. The first voice calls upon another sense, hearing, and pronounces nature to be bobolink, sea, thunder, cricket; whereupon the second voice comes back with, "Harmony." Harmony may be composed of elements apprehended with the sense of hearing, but the mind must order them for there to be "Harmony."

So far the idea that nature is beyond the self, is physical and object, is therefore apprehended by humans through our senses, has been contrasted to the idea that nature is more than that, is what the mind does with objects through interpretation and abstraction. (Up to this point the poem has nowhere denied the existence of the outside world; the concepts "Heaven" and "Harmony" are based upon those objects that the senses encounter. The argument is about meaning.)

Now another set of four lines complete the poem, beginning, as did the earlier two, with "Nature is." What voice is speaking? This third unit looks parallel to the others but is not entirely, because no second voice comes in in the last line to dispute the statements of a first. Let us call the third voice not a brand-new speaker but a composite of voices one and two that, combined, create a third. The third voice describes a situation which contains both positions, that nature is out there and that the mind's interpretation is also real, and extends them into further insight. The third voice's argument is based upon the idea that nature is what we know; *know* parallels in its position *see* and *hear,* but it represents the cognitive perception implied by *Heaven* and *Harmony* as much or even more than it does sensory perception. It denotes most accurately a combination of the two. Finally, we might wish to note that the mind's propensity to abstract, as portrayed by voice two, is also demonstrated, willy nilly, in the language of voice one, the exponent of all that is concrete, when it includes *afternoon* in its list of things in nature. We may be seeing already in the supposed antithesis the implicit synthesis.

The concluding voice continues the pattern of the beginning with a definition of nature; this one pauses after one line but is not finished. "Nature is what we know – Yet have no art to say –" is the complete thought. *Know,* as I have just said, most certainly includes the mind in the fact of nature. *Know* demands perception, both cognitive and sensory; so that whatever nature is, its meaning is invested in the mind's perception of it. What we know but have no art to say: a new and necessary distinction has been made between thought and expression, suddenly making this a poem about poetry as well. It is one thing to perceive nature, quite another to tell what it is (the purpose of this poem). Why? The concluding lines explain. Knowledge is paralleled by "Wisdom" and juxtaposed against nature's "Simplicity." In the light of that simplicity, our wisdom is impotent, powerless. To say, that is. If the poem to this point has been giving all the points, all the importance, to the mind in its transaction with nature, now we get the other side. It is the mind which sees pattern in sound to create harmony, but it needs the objects that make sound with which to work. Further, the mind has to work at meaning, while the objects are simply there. They demonstrate the articulateness of sheer embodiment that the mind does not possess. How to talk about this? The minute that the mind grants meaning to objects, turns bobolink and thunder into harmony, it fails to express what Dickinson will call in another poem the "Object Absolute."

In chapter 1 I spoke of how the mind can include nature within its perimeters because it can think about nature. That is one way in which the mind is analogous to nature. The mind is also like nature because through perception it creates meaning for nature: "The Outer – from the Inner / Derives its Magnitude –" (451). Nevertheless, nature is there; it has an existence of its own and is not a projection of the mind. Its acts can be analogous to the mind's acts, because both exist in this world. But mind and nature are not exact versions of one another. The mind possesses the creative power of the imagination; nature does not. Nature in turn possesses the simplicity of embodiment uncomplicated by meaning; the mind does not. Therefore in trying to speak of these relationships the poet may begin with the parallelism that her analogies project, but she will consistently have to "explode" it in order that her language might thereby approximate the true and complex situation.[12] Our wisdom may struggle with impotence, but one of the tasks that Dickinson set herself was precisely that of making an art which could say.

3

Analogy, parallelism, and aphorism are language features that extend and expand in the various forms that I have been describing; but their components are individual words, the vocabulary that I have separated into two strands: dimensional and conceptual. Next I should like to examine more closely dimension and concept as they function in definitions of mental experience.

We have already observed that the primary source for the dimensional vocabulary, used to show how mental acts take up space, occur in time, is the natural world.

> No Man can compass a Despair—
> As round a Goalless Road
> No faster than a Mile at once
> The Traveller proceed—
>
> Unconscious of the Width—
> Unconscious that the Sun
> Be setting on His progress—
> So accurate the One
>
> At estimating Pain—
> Whose own—has just begun—
> His ignorance—the Angel
> That pilot Him along—
>
> [477]

Despair is a mental state, an emotion. To seek to measure it is an impulse which grants to that emotion a condition of dimension. The analogy upon which this poem is structured further defines the kind of dimension that despair occupies in the space of the mind.

These boundaries are not so simple to chart. Although this poem offers a concrete example for an abstraction, the example is negative, because the act of measuring a despair is impossible. Nevertheless, lack of boundary is also an aspect of dimension.

The poem's first word, "No," initiates the negative rhetoric upon which the entire statement is based. The negative is a difficult construction: it gives, then takes away, in order to show with language (which is) what is not. "No Man can compass a Despair—" is the opening aphorism, followed by an analogy, drawn from the world of nature, to help explain this truism. That is, "road" comes from the world outside the mind, but what about "goalless"? For this is a road that doesn't go anywhere, doesn't get anywhere, never ends. At the very outset the neatness of the analogy is exploded, because such a road never did exist in nature and is the mind's work only. The vocabulary of this analogy, its *road, mile, traveler, width, sun,* and *progress,* gives concrete dimension to the image, the depiction of what happens along this road. But that experiential concreteness belongs to the wrong experience, which is the point of the analogy. The man travelling on a goalless road is aware only of the individual moment, the individual mile, and can*not* see its actual width, is *not* aware of the totality of time that passes. His experience of this road is not of a goalless road but of an ordinary road: so much the better for him.

As, so determines the form of analogical structure here. As the man on a goalless road, so the person trying to measure pain. Just "so" accurate: i.e., inaccurate. The negative again, couched in the form of the positive. The complete poem plays the inaccuracy of the concrete against the accuracy of the abstract in order to make a case for ignorance and lack of a fully realized consciousness. For ordinary people, anyway. The poet knows, of course, or she couldn't tell.

The concluding line of stanza two and the first line of stanza three return to the poem's first line by paralleling it, "So accurate the One / At estimating Pain—," then giving further details of the situation: "Whose own—has just begun—." It is important that we understand how the impulse to measure comes at the beginning of the condition. The person entering upon despair wants to know how far, how long it extends. And this is why his very ignorance is his better guide in the situation, his pilot angel. The last two lines of the poem turn, with their metaphor, back into the analogical situation of the goalless road, thereby conflating tenor and vehicle. Because if the man starting the journey, the man commencing despair understood that perceived dimension was actually non-dimension, that the experience to be encountered had *no limits,* he might well go mad from the knowledge. This possibility is implicit in the poem rather than explicit, but it is there on the other side of the negative concrete that is offered for rhetoric. The other side is the existence of what Dickinson calls in another poem "Illocality" (963), although there is no direct vocabulary for describing it. Of course there isn't, because the natural world, the primary source for words of dimension, is located. And while the poet is keen on indicating that the mind, likewise, is occupied space, there are other aspects of the mind that are limitless, without boundary. The extent and duration of despair is one of these.

Talking about the extremes or edges of dimension requires concept, the abstract.

> A nearness to Tremendousness –
> An Agony procures –
> Affliction ranges Boundlessness –
> Vicinity to Laws
>
> Contentment's quiet Suburb –
> Affliction cannot stay
> In Acres – Its Location
> Is Illocality –

[963]

This companion poem to "No Man can compass a Despair" is also concerned with situation and boundaries of emotional events, but it presents a different attitude towards the subject, admiring instead of fearing illocality. In its discussion of agony the poem develops by means of analogical progression. What is almost missing here, however, is the concrete vocabulary that we associate with analogy. There is some but not much: what isn't there along with what is demonstrates some boundaries of the issue of boundary.

Specifically, agony, although treated in terms of the space that it occupies, requires for its description an abstract vocabulary, while its opposite, contentment, is allotted concrete imagery. Contentment is or possesses, inhabits, a quiet suburb, a region near or adjacent to or structured by "Laws." Context helps in determining what is meant here by "Laws." Placed in direct contrast to "Boundlessness," it seems to connote the opposite—that which creates boundaries, what rules do. *Suburb* is concrete; so is *Acres,* where affliction couldn't stay but by implication contentment could. Agony's terrain, on the other hand, is near to tremendousness, moving freely over boundlessness: for location, lack of it.

In other words, although *nearness, ranges, vicinity, stay,* and *location* make clear the fact that this poem is about the space an emotion occupies, these words are used to help develop a theme showing how certain emotions, like agony or affliction, are of such depth, width, intensity, profundity, that they must occupy mental space without boundaries. To denote those places that are really non-places the abstractions which we associate with the conceptual vocabulary are required.

Tremendousness and *Boundlessness* are two such abstractions. Tremendousness has aspects of place because one can be near it; on the other hand, its abstract form labels it as the idea of great size, not a specific instance of it. Boundlessness, likewise capable of being ranged, is in some sense there; on the other hand, as the idea of no boundaries, there is another sense in which it is not there. In contrast to the opening two parallel and analogous statements about the relationship between extreme emotion and extreme space are lines four and five, bridging the two stanzas, narrowing in the mental field with their vocabulary of closeness and domesticity. We have been shown point (twice) and counterpoint. Conclusion comes with a final analogue, in lines six through eight, which rephrases the statements about agony and affliction with which the poem began but uses both vocabularies in doing so. Development and closure comes from the fact that both thesis and antithesis (abstract and concrete) have been used to make the final aphorism. It has its own double or parallel structure: a negation followed by its positive version. The negation cannot help but imply the opposite position: affliction can't stay in concrete space, i.e., acres (because, as we know, it demands abstract space). Then the final paradox, based directly upon the tension between abstract and concrete in operation throughout: agony's location is therefore no location. There is a location that is not a location, and that is abstract space rather than concrete space, a space which must therefore be mental space.

In describing emotional experience, Dickinson needs to be able to point to the feature of mental space that I discussed earlier when speaking of her outer-spatial metaphors for the mind: the vastness and lack of boundaries when space is idea, is conceptual space. For this task words drawn not from nature but from thought, abstractions, are required.

Time is the other dimension delineating mental experience. In these poems time and space are aspects of one another.

> There is a pain – so utter –
> It swallows substance up –

Then covers the Abyss with Trance –
So Memory can step
Around – across – upon it –
As one within a Swoon –
Goes safely – where an open eye –
Would drop Him – Bone by Bone.

[599]

The intensity and completeness of the pain described in this poem is conveyed with a spatial vocabulary. Incorporating all other experience within itself, such pain leaves a huge hole where everything else was. That hole is then covered over by another state of mind, trance, into which, if one stayed totally conscious (to translate the metaphors), one would fall and, like everything else, be swallowed up.

Time as well as distance is a component of these first-aid tactics, as the continuation of the metaphor into lines five and six reveals. Once the hole of pain is covered with the lid of trance, memory can cross the place without having to encounter the pain. In other words, there is a period of time immediately after the occurrence of great pain when the mind seals off this particular part of itself from itself in order to be able to function at all. (In "After great pain, a formal feeling comes –," poem 341, Dickinson is describing that same emergency procedure with other metaphors. "The Hour of Lead," she calls it, telling us in that poem what happens later: "Remembered, if outlived / As Freezing persons, recollect the Snow – / First – Chill – then Stupor – then the letting go –.") This poem is about the chill and the stupor; the letting go occurs in some undocumented future.

After developing this little allegory, the poem proceeds to analogy in its final three lines. This situation is like, we are told, what happens when someone in a swoon goes in safety, whereas total consciousness, an open eye, "Would drop Him – Bone by Bone." Goes where? Fall into what? To what death? The poem stops without answering these questions, and Dickinson does not establish the parallel circumstances in the outer world where a state of swoon would allow a traveller to proceed in safety and bypass some hole. No, because this analogy is repetition rather than comparison, repetition for the sake of emphasis. It's the same trance, the same hole, the same danger, and it takes place in the same mind. The primary analogy in the poem has been already created, in an extreme version, that of allegory, in its first story: the discussion of hole, lid, and traveller. It is simply rephrased at the poem's conclusion, but so that it ends with an image not of safety but of the terrible danger that must be avoided: falling into the hole. The chilling, frightening quality of "Bone by Bone" parallels and elucidates the very first line of the poem, "There is a pain – so utter –."

Time's activities within the mind, in particular those of memory, are documented here, as one stage in a process for coping is described. Language embodies time by rendering its actions with a concrete vocabulary of spatial dimension.

The explicit interconnection between time and space in mental activity is the theme of the following poem.

> Pain – expands the Time –
> Ages coil within
> The minute Circumference
> Of a single Brain –
>
> Pain contracts – the Time –
> Occupied with Shot
> Gamuts of Eternities
> Are as they were not –
>   [967]

Some of Dickinson's poems, as we have seen, find analogous situations between mind and world; some, like this one, make their point by explicitly differentiating the two realms. Time as it functions here, within the space of the mind, overcomes so-called natural laws. Within the brain it expands and contracts as it does not do in nature. To show this, Dickinson relies upon a dimensional vocabulary. Time is pictured as a tape, now coiled, now uncoiled, taking up significant space in the brain.

What makes time different to and in the brain is the experience of pain. While "There is a pain – so utter –" describes pain as precursor to a necessary lack of sensation, this poem focuses upon pain's propensity to heighten sensation. In pain, rather than directly after it, one's sense of time is "expanded": each moment seems intensified to an abnormal degree, so that "ages" are experienced. On the other hand, pain can cause one's sense of time to become selective (contracted), as pain creates moments of supreme intensity, "Shot," upon which one focuses to the exclusion of other less significant and therefore less fully realized moments.

In making its case for a different sense of time, the poem carefully contrasts a description of the physical brain—"The minute Circumference / Of a single Brain"—with an equally physical, dimensional set of images for time: ages that are coiled within, gamuts of eternity. Insisting on a physiognomical view of the mind, insisting likewise that time takes up space, the poem forces us to see that there is another kind of circumference involved. Its measurements are determined by the mind's view of itself, by perception.

Mental experience like pain affects perception, the poem says. Perception controls the rolling up, the rolling out of time. This poem develops out of the philosophy also expressed in " 'Nature' is what we see –," the idea that although things exist out there in nature—time does—it is the mind that grants meaning to it.

"Two Lengths has every Day," Dickinson writes: "Its absolute extent / And Area superior / By Hope or Horror lent" (1295). This is because, as another poem explains in more detail:

> Perception of an object costs
> Precise the Object's loss –
> Perception in itself a Gain
> Replying to its Price –
>
> The Object Absolute – is nought –
> Perception sets it fair
> And then upbraids a Perfectness
> That situates so far –
>
> [1071]

"Absolute" is the essential word in both the quotation and the full poem, because it is the word Dickinson uses for the nature that exists without benefit of perception. Absolute can mean pure, total, ultimate, intrinsic; free from limit or restriction or qualification; determined in itself and not by anything outside itself. The mind may seek to obtain for itself such pureness, but it never can, since the mind's relation to the world is precisely that of qualifier. The mind is what is outside the object. On the other hand, the mind can understand that it is exactly its own "impurity" which is interesting and significant. While the quotation from "Two Lengths has every day" opts for the latter attitude, "Perception of an object costs" discusses them both.

In the quotation, "absolute" is contrasted to "superior." Superiority is granted to the natural world, the time / space dimension of day, by perception, which is in turn influenced in its decisions by the mind's emotional situation, by hope or horror. Nevertheless, two lengths exist for the day, simultaneously, and both are real.

The first stanza of poem 1071 more carefully explores this seeming paradox with a financial vocabulary of investment, profits, loss, and gain. To perceive the object is to lose it, announces aphorism number one. But, continues aphorism number two, though the object is lost, perception is itself a gain. "Replying to its price": the gain is in direct ratio to the price paid. That is, when the mind perceives an object, the object cannot be the object as it was without the perception—determined in itself and not by anything outside itself. That object, what she will call in the second stanza the "Object Absolute," is forever lost. But what is gained in the process, by means of the loss of the object absolute (the price paid) is the meaning of the object: "Area superior / By Hope or Horror lent."

Perhaps because the first stanza has been so enigmatic, the poem provides a second stanza, one more aphorism, for explanation. That the second is more difficult to interpret than the first may be a further indication of the thorough complexity of the issue raised. (Or it may be more simply that Dickinson herself would see no difficulty at all in her language, nor would she expect the reader to; provided, of course, that the ear be not too dull.) In stanza two the idea of the object absolute is introduced and immediately declared to be "nought." It is all perception's fault, for believing in the first place that the object absolute could be a potential possession. Perception puts the highest price on it, to revert to the original metaphor, then gets angry with the object because it has been set at such a cost that it is unobtainable. Perception ought rather upbraid itself. Perception understands that the idea of the object absolute is the idea of an object existing without the presence of perception, then wants to possess it anyway. Nevertheless, it is important that although the mind cannot possess the pure object and, as the first stanza has maintained, there is even benefit in that situation, the mind can imagine the idea of the object absolute. (The mind has set it fair, called it perfect, situated it far.) In that way, in the space of the mind only (and in the companion space of the poem), a kind of possession is enacted, and it is an instance of the special way in which the brain is wider than the sky, deeper than the sea, just the weight of God.[13]

In the mind, dimension and concept are necessarily aspects of one another. Although I have identified two vocabularies, the dimensional and the conceptual, they fit together to form the language of poems about mental experience. Talking about dimension itself requires both concrete and abstract words: both association with the natural world and acknowledgment of the peculiar aspects of mental space. Equally, poems about mental events showing special interest in their conceptual elements need dimension for clarification.

> Love – is anterior to Life –
> Posterior – to Death –
> Initial of Creation, and
> The Exponent of Earth –
> [917]

Anterior, posterior—these words indicate that love, in this one-aphorism poem, is being defined dimensionally in terms of time and space. Life and death, however, are not places but concepts. Love, occurring before life begins and after the conclusion that is death, transcends all human or natural space and time. The love being discussed, then, is not a particular instance of the emotion but the idea of it. (We may consider substituting Divine Love here for the idea of love, since human love can be seen as a type for God's love, but to make the poem expressly religious seems unnecessary. For Dickinson the two concepts are usually interchangeable, each a workable metaphor for the other.) Consequently, we see from its opening two lines that this poem is situated in conceptual space, where terms of dimension are necessary guidelines to meaning but have little to do with space in nature.

The poem continues to define further the position and hence significance of love. "Initial of Creation" may be simply paraphrasing "anterior to Life," but initial has other meanings besides first. It can mean the first letter—of the word, "Creation." Not literally—love is not the letter c—but symbolically, love standing for the force that compels creation: of individuals, of the world.

Even as love is both first and last, it is both cause and effect. It is the "Exponent of Earth"; example, symbolic representation (the symbol, in fact, for repetition), of the world. It is therefore a primary force, encompassing life, death, all that is in between, and all that is beyond.

A poem about idea, this epigram makes it clear that idea does not exist in a vacuum, as it maps with precision love's situation.

At first glance the next and final poem does not look as if it belongs in this series. It appears to be a poem about nature itself, about prairies. But by the end of the first line we begin to understand that once again action is set in the mind and not somewhere in Kansas, that in this recipe we are concerned with prairie-ness and not an instance of it.

> To make a prairie it takes a clover and one bee,
> One clover, and a bee,
> And revery.
> The revery alone will do,
> If bees are few.

[1755]

Although the poem's vocabulary is concrete enough—*prairie, clover,* and *bee*—the statement made in the opening line is, upon reflection, absurd. No actual prairie consists of a clover and one bee. However, the following line, emphasizing through repetition the importance to the formula of clover and bee, also points to their representative nature. Yet with the inclusion, as the sentence ends, of the abstract *revery* into this prescription for prairie-ness, we might well be startled. For what has revery to do with prairies? And where would one put it, how next to clover and bee? If we are not quite so literal, we can understand how the sensation of seeing a prairie might be similar to the feeling of revery: a dream-like beauty, epitomized by the scent of a flower, the drone of a bee. Practically, for Dickinson to make a prairie, she has to do it in her mind: she has never seen a prairie and probably does not need to see one. For her to make a prairie, revery—i.e., imagination—is necessary. Necessary and sufficient, as the conclusion of the poem announces, with some humor: "The revery alone will do, / If bees are few."

To make. This poem, when set alongside " 'Nature' is what we see –" and "Perception of an object costs," defines the mind's creativity in its relations with the world. A prairie in the world of nature cannot be composed from one clover and one bee, but the idea of prairie can. A prairie in the mind. Another kind of real. In this poem Dickinson uses the existence of clovers and bees in nature as source for her revery; yet she also insists that the revery alone will do. Which comes first, we are tempted to ask: idea or thing? Neither, we can surmise from the evidence of these poems and also from "Love – is anterior to Life –." Idea and thing exist in simultaneous, interdependent relationship, as do the conceptual and dimensional vocabularies in Dickinson's poems on the subject of mental experience. There is an object absolute, but there is also the idea of an object absolute. The mind's idea of a given object creates it, makes it, insofar as, through the act of perception, mind provides object with meaning. And, since the mind can also think of an object that is unperceived, it in that sense creates it before perception. It can think of love before, after life: in this fashion it can create idea before object. Each idea is a creation. If it is the idea of an object, then the object is created by the idea. In the mind, if not in the world. And in the poem.

When, in "'Nature' is what we see –," Dickinson speaks of creating harmony from bobolink, sea, thunder, and cricket, she is using an abstract word to show the conceptual power of the mind. In "To make a prairie" she uses a concrete word, *prairie,* for the same purpose. In the mind, abstract and concrete partake of one another: abstract has dimension: concrete is representative. This helps to explain a peculiar and often noticed quality of Dickinson's use of abstract and concrete words. Abstract words seem so concrete: see *Tremendousness, nearness to; Creation, Initial of.* Concrete words turn out to be abstract: see *Road, Goalless; Suburb, Contentment's Quiet.* Especially, through a frequent and thorough use of metaphors based upon a structure of analogy, the interaction between these linguistic opposites is effected. "Faith – is the Pierless Bridge"; "Presentiment – is that long Shadow – on the Lawn –"; "The Suburbs of a Secret." Metaphor, as in these first lines of poems, renders abstract concrete, concrete abstract; not annihilating differences but underlining relationship.

A rare ear not too dull may be one requirement for telling, but another is constructing the art to say. To make the prairie that is revery Dickinson uses dimensional and conceptual vocabularies that connect in structures of analogy, patterns of parallelism, modes of aphorism. These features of language combine to create poems that can articulate the shape and meaning of mental experience.

iii *"Peril as a Possession"*

WHEN DICKINSON DESCRIBES mental experience in her poems, those acts that take place in the space of the mind, her procedure is one of measurement. It is essential for her to have these experiences—the more intense, the better; and it is equally essential that they be documented, mapped, measured. Measuring through the medium of poetry is what allows her to engage in intensest experience and to use it profitably.

This chapter looks at one extreme of emotion, pain, and at the ways in which Dickinson claims pain as her subject. Her poems show that pain must be experienced, because it leads to insight, to knowledge. Moreover, pain is valuable in its own right: it brings one more fully alive. It has dangers, however, both physical and mental. Pushed too far, it can cause actual death and also psychic death, which is despair. But pain can be controlled with measurement; Dickinson's gauge is words. Control is essential to achieve, because control is power.

Dickinson's poetic language defines pain by circling it, surrounding it, and thereby isolating it. The shape at the center is clarified by filling in the shapes that surround it. Measurement is a process of circumference. Circumference demands dimension, and Dickinson uses time and space as rhetorical strategies. To reveal the presence of pain, she writes of before its arrival and after its departure, so that time offers a perspective on its nature. Poems from within its present tense are the most difficult. They, too, require some kind of perspective to achieve validity; they find it in a spatial rhetoric. Analogies complicated by metaphor measure pain by forming and denying correlations with the outside world of physical experience. When she is finished—in one poem, in series of poems which approach from many directions this same subject, pain, like a wild beast, has been encircled, imprisoned, and possessed in a net of words.

Although relationship and lack of it between mind and world are especially at issue when the subject is pain, Dickinson's poems do not look to autobiography to establish contact with, foundation in, the external world. Danger, crisis, agony, grief, despair about *what*? The poems are not concerned with what—nor with who, where, or when. The affairs of the world are jumping-off places for the leap into the complex tides of the mind, but that is all. The analogies the poems make are to sensation, not stimulus. Robert Weisbuch comments upon the "classificatory" nature of Dickinson's activities in these poems. "Dickinson casts about furiously to describe the horror of these moments," he writes, "not their cause, and their stated plurality, like the plurality of analogous images, tends towards law and away from situation."[1] This is what I am calling measurement: the laws towards which her poems tend, yet another version of her aphoristic mode, create control over this most dangerous of materials, danger itself, by providing description and rules for its behavior.

Yet Dickinson does not appear to eschew autobiography because she distrusts the personal, because she wishes to generalize and hence escape or validate private experience. Her poems about pain are as personal as they are, in fact, universal: Dickinson has created a "universal of the personal" that is especially characteristic of women writers.[2] When she writes of pain, its sensations and its events, she is documenting the most personal and private of experiences, none other. She has not checked her texts of philosophy or religion: her data is her own. She is in this sense as "confessional" as Anne Sexton.

Nevertheless, the fact that these poems lack all reference to people and places makes them distinctive. Why would she prefer personal psychology to personal history? I think that the answer is related to a burning issue in Dickinson's life, the matter of control and power. Even as she chooses the life of the mind to obtain and maintain control over her life, so she can control pain through verbal measures much more successfully than through personal interaction. Her biographer, Richard Sewall, defines her "hiding" as follows:

If it can be said that she hid herself from her friends to understand friendship, to create in her imagination the divine street the lover travels, so in her search for the essence of everything that came within her consciousness, she hid herself to write her poems—and (for whatever reason) hid her poems, except for a few. In a world of process and evanescence, to which the bulk of her poems testify, the only way left to her was to construct permanences of the mind. . . .[3]

The safety or distance that the world of the mind grants makes possible the different kinds of risk and involvement which characterize her self-appointed work.

1

"Her best poetry," writes Charles Anderson, "is not concerned with the causes but with the qualities of pain. . . . The qualities she sought to fix with greatest precision are its intensity, its duration, and the change it brings about."[4] Weisbuch concurs: "Dickinson strives to measure the imagination rather than to claim everything for it, and she wants it to earn its way, by suffering."[5]

> Peril as a Possession
> 'Tis Good to bear
> Danger Disintegrates Satiety
> There's Basis there—
> Begets an awe
> That searches Human Nature's creases
> As clean as Fire.
> [1678]

This is one of several poems showing why one would seek out peril or danger on purpose. The paradoxical nature of its theme (for how can peril, wild, be a posession, tame?) is resolved in moral terms: "Good" and "Basis." Two interlocking sequences in apposition to the phrase "Peril as a Possession" define means and results.

The appearance of danger on the mental scene is like that of some adventurer with a fiery weapon that destroys the underbrush of complacency, the lethargy of surfeit. This cleansing annihilation provides "Basis," the cleared ground upon which the experience of peril can be enacted. That experience is long, demanding patience, suffering. For peril must be borne, and this brings good. (Another description of this same event comes to mind: "Power is only Pain—/

Stranded, thro' Discipline,/Till Weights–will hang–" [252]. These lines point to the necessity of endurance—"Stranded"; also to the means, "Discipline," and the result, "Power.")

"Peril as a Possession" is also the understood subject of the last three lines. Whereas lines two through four clarify peril, its effects on the mind and the mind's effects on it, the last three lines proceed from possession to document its results. Bearing pain is the means of possessing it; the fear that comes from the possession of peril is not terror but awe, an heightened appreciation that brings with it vision or insight. It is described with a metaphor following from the image of danger as a weapon, something like a laser beam, that "searches Human Nature's creases/As clean as Fire." The insight of awe is a piercing virtue and purifies through simplification. The "creases" of human nature, of the mind, are flattened, their shadows and complications reduced to essence. Purity and pain become aspects of one another, as the concluding simile reveals in its juxtaposition of "clean" and "fire."

Peril may be dangerous and fiery, but bearing it brings it to heel so that it can be utilized on behalf of good. The danger itself is not reduced, however, by its possession. For fear and pain are necessary to disintegrate satiety, to force the mind to extremity. But possession does bring control, thus power. The good is not in the bearing by itself but in the knowledge to which it can lead.

With its active interchange between concept and dimension, this poem insists upon the spatial nature of mental events. Danger is shown affecting the configuration of its environment: disintegrating satiety, uncovering basis, begetting an awe that searches human nature's creases. At the same time, the mind, learning to bear peril and finally to possess it, has an effect upon its form.

> I lived on Dread–
> To Those who know
> The Stimulus there is
> In Danger–Other impetus
> Is numb–and Vitalless–
>
> As 'twere a Spur–upon the Soul–
> A Fear will urge it where
> To go without the Spectre's aid
> Were Challenging Despair.
>   [770]

This poem, too, believes in the significant results of danger. Here a metaphor of motion, of journey, is used; although the goal, journey's end, is referred to only as "where." The poem's focus, however, is neither on the awe nor on the suffering involved in the experience of dread; its concern is less with discipline and more with the excitement that is engendered. The poem helps us to see how someone who never explored Antarctica, or even New York City, might find food for an adventurous spirit.

Three parallel phrases in the first stanza link to define the experience of dread: "I lived on Dread"; "The Stimulus there is / In Danger"; "Other impetus / Is numb – and Vitalless –." The first phrase identifies dread with sustenance, a total diet: one you can live on. The following phrases show why. "Danger" parallels "Dread": they are synonymous; "stimulus" explains the nature of the substance "lived on." "Impetus" is yet another word for it: these terms point to both immediate energy and future purpose. Finally, the third phrase invokes the negative to reveal dread's positive superiority. Anything else is "numb," "Vitalless." Dread gives rise to sensation and makes one feel alive.

Parallelism of definition in stanza one is reinforced by analogical structure in stanza two: concepts are given concrete form. Dread, or danger, is like a spur—which makes the soul, what it is spurring, like a horse. The image of spur urging horse again evokes motion and a sense of direction; the complementary analogy in the final three lines at last mentions its direction, the "where." One more synonym for dread and danger is added, fear—in apposition to spur, so that the concrete analogue for an abstract state has been abstracted right back into mind space. The spur of fear will urge the soul, but "where" is described indirectly, in terms of its own implicit risks. If one were to go there without danger as the impetus ("the spectre" is one more synonym for dread, and the sharp pressure of the spur is suddenly seen as "aid"), that would be "Challenging Despair." The lack of danger's presence would mean the presence of despair. And this, according to the poem, is a greater danger than danger.

Although the poem to this point has insisted upon a synonymic parallelism between its terms for a mental condition—Dread, Stimulus, Danger, Impetus, Spur, Fear, Spectre, now it draws a subtle but severe distinction between states or versions of pain. This is one purpose for poetry: as measurement, it points out significant similarities and differences. At the conclusion of this poem an important difference is posited, one which we have encountered before: "the difference between Despair/And Fear" (305). Poem 305 revealed the passive impotence of despair ("when the Wreck has been") as compared to the active distress of fear ("the instant of a Wreck"). "I lived on Dread" has all along insisted upon the vitality of danger and its corollary sensations, dread and fear. Despair, on the other hand, is a kind of living death, "contented" (that frightening word) "as the Eye/Upon the Forehead of a Bust –/That knows – it cannot see –." Dickinson's own dictionary defined despair as the extremest form of pain, resulting in hopelessness, though with only subordinate theological connotations; that is, loss of hope in the mercy of God.[6]

Thus "I lived on Dread" distinguishes between the life-giving effect of danger—as stimulus to insight, to vision or knowledge, achievable only when the soul is pushed to extreme places (insists, too, that the very ride itself, a journey to discovery, is truest living and should be undertaken, because of what she calls in poem 1581 "the obligation/to Electricity") and the death-like effects of despair, a condition intrinsic to those far places at the edge of the mind.

> The Soul's distinct connection
> With immortality
> Is best disclosed by Danger
> Or quick Calamity –
>
> As Lightning on a Landscape
> Exhibits Sheets of Place –
> Not yet suspected – but for Flash –
> And Click – and Suddenness.
> [974]

The "where" of "I lived on Dread" is here revealed to be immortality. In a subsequent chapter I shall examine the connection between vision or insight and immortality that has been predicated by this series of poems on danger. Here immortality is named as the object of vision, as a place "Not yet suspected" but there.

It is danger, or quick calamity, that uncovers the soul's connection with immortality, so an opening aphorism announces, indicating that this is a poem about purpose, about the mental traveller's reward for experiencing danger.

Analogy supplements aphorism with an image of discovery that also reveals something about the journey. The comparison appears to be between mind and world—the soul's connection with immortality is like "Lightning on a Landscape." But where or when the landscape is is not explained, because it is not the place but rather the angle of vision that is at issue. The way in which lightning discloses "Sheets of Place" (*sheets* links the way of seeing with what is seen, evoking both place's stretch or expanse and lightning's sharp edges) is similar to the way in which, in poem 1678, awe "searches Human Nature's creases / As clean as Fire." The "Flash," "Click," and "Suddenness" of the lightning causes revelation: the fiery sharp ray or beam of insight that shares its attributes with the pain and fear that danger as a condition engenders. The landscape of immortality is "disclosed" but has been there all along, even as the "Basis" present when danger disintegrates satiety is not created but revealed. It is as if there are two scapes for the same land; what changes is not so much shapes but their meaning.

The journey here is not the slow plodding of suffering, bearing, of pain "stranded, thro' Discipline / Till Weights – will hang –." Nor is it a wild horse ride; rather, it is a sudden, total shift in vision. Now you didn't see it; now you do. Sometimes, in Dickinson's canon of poems about the achievement of vision, one has to work at it, sometimes it is a gift; sometimes both go together. In this poem, danger, like lightning, is an environmental condition without which the discovery might not occur.

The poem's two stanzas are analogous, so that the parallelism of their components indicates the nature of the relationship between soul and immortality. Lightning parallels danger, landscape parallels soul, and sheets of place parallels immortality. The sheets of place, as we have seen, are not a different place but a part of the same landscape. Lightning alters one's perception of it. So, immortality is revealed by danger to be an aspect of the soul, which we know to be another kind of landscape. Immortality is, likewise, not out there but in here, and the way to see it has more to do with an angle of vision than with death.

Dickinson's poems about danger show why it is a necessary condition for the most significant experience. But she is equally aware that danger is dangerous. On the one hand, it is life-enriching: it provokes energy, excitement, "Electricity," and leads to knowledge. But if pushed too far, it brings death: the psychic death that is despair; and literal death as well.

The hallowing of Pain
Like hallowing of Heaven,
Obtains at a corporeal cost –
The Summit is not given

To Him who strives severe
At middle of the Hill –
But He who has achieved the Top –
All – is the price of All –

[772]

This is a poem about ultimates: what they offer and what they cost. Its subject is not just pain but its worship, a way to arrive at ultimate pain. This act is paralleled, in the opening two lines, with the more usual worship of Heaven (and compared, through an implicit pun, to the harrowing of Hell). Thus evil and good, pain and pleasure, are linked analogically, so that the meaning of "cost" might better be understood. Particularly, "corporeal cost": mental experience is in no way divorced from the body.

The opening three lines form an aphorism, and they are parallelled by another analogy, then another, summarizing, aphorism. All three units of the poem are synonymous to one another and thereby establish definition.

The second analogy—to climb, hill, and summit—is predictable in terms of the first, the comparison between the hallowing of pain and the hallowing of Heaven. Heaven is conventionally at the top of the hill of life, up which the good Christian climbs. He attains the summit, or heaven, at a corporeal cost which, in this instance, is none other than death.

But this analogy is not present to explain the hallowing of Heaven (proper religious conduct) but, rather, the hallowing of pain. Which the good Christian should not be engaged in. Bearing it, yes, but not worshipping it. Then it becomes closer to hell than to heaven, more like evil than good. In Christianity's view, if not Emily Dickinson's. What she wishes to show is that pain yields its best rewards exactly as does religion, through complete and thorough devotion. And pain, as these analogies indicate, is equally worth the endeavor. Pain is another kind of summit—attainment, culmination. It, too, we understand when we follow the analogy through, demands "corporeal cost": can—might—must?—require death.

For "All – is the price of All –," maintains the concluding aphorism in its hyperbolic simplicity. The first *all* stands for what you give, the second for what you get: in the realm of ultimates, these become the same. Ultimate pain is shown to be as desirable, and as demanding, as ultimate good. Ultimate anything requires the ultimate from one who would have it. Through the entire poem weaves a vocabulary of financial transaction that complements its spiritual component: achievement is always as pragmatic as it is transcendent. *Cost, given, achieved, price:* when the stakes are this high, something must be ransomed.

As Dickinson's use of the same word for goal and price indicates, ultimates partake of one another. For example, in achieving ultimate sensation one may arrive at the edge and be forced over, into the ultimate end of sensation, which is death. Yet striving "severe / At middle of the hill" gets one nowhere. Only propelling the self towards summit, top, *all,* only hallowing pain, will permit the fullest experience of it.

Pain at its ultimate risks the twin deaths of despair and mortality ("corporeal cost"). Crisis marks the moment when the edge is reached. In poem 948, for example, "'Twas Crisis—All the length had passed—," crisis is viewed as a moment as brief as it is fierce:

> The instant holding in its claw
> The privilege to live
> Or warrant to report the Soul
> The other side the Grave.

In this poem the poised moment of crisis gives way to death.

> The Second poised – debated – shot –
> Another had begun –
> And simultaneously, a Soul
> Escaped the House unseen –

Crisis is, finally, so interesting because it is as thin, as delicate, and, perhaps, as bright as a hair, "at the edge of the territory of death and eternity but not in it," as Weisbuch comments. It is a vantage point from which one can see into the meaning of things, yet from which one may just as easily fall into the end of things. This is the ultimate risk of crisis, that it occurs precisely at the interface between vision and conclusion, which may be why this last poem is read by Albert Gelpi as "death scene" and by Robert Weisbuch as about the idea that "the slightest further movement of the mind will allow eternity to present itself in the realm of this life."[7]

> Crisis is a Hair
> Toward which the forces creep
> Past which forces retrograde
> If it come in sleep
>
> To suspend the Breath
> Is the most we can
> Ignorant is it Life or Death
> Nicely balancing.
>
> Let an instant push
> Or an Atom press
> Or a Circle hesitate
> In Circumference
>
> It – may jolt the Hand
> That adjusts the Hair
> That secures Eternity
> From presenting – Here –
>   [889]

Concentrating upon the nature of the balance itself, the poem is, in my opinion, purposely ambiguous about what happens afterwards. "The forces" which both creep toward it and may withdraw from it are identified as "Life or Death," but which is not specified. Eternity is prevented, by the presence of the hair, from entering the present, but nowhere in the poem is eternity identified with death. All we know is that it exists on one side or the other of crisis.

The poem's focus on the nature of the balance tells us something about control as well as loss of control. The self may not know the outcome of crisis (that very ignorance is surely part of what makes the tightrope act so frightening), but it alone—the mind or consciousness—is what keeps the hair in place. The poem contrasts the experience of crisis in sleep and awake. In sleep, the forces that have crept toward the hair will "retrograde": withdraw, degenerate. Then there is no stopping the process, and "retrograde," with its connotations of decline, seems to promise death. Yet the second stanza proposes suspending the breath as the appropriate response to crisis ("the most we can"). Holding one's breath is not the same as being unable to breathe. It is a self-induced pause, a suspension, rather than an externally induced termination. It is not death but a pause or poise during which sensibility is at once stretched and still, like the hair.

The slightest alteration in time or space may disrupt the balance, as Dickinson's examples indicate: "instant"; "Atom." The paradoxical natue of the balance is also revealed: it is movement as well as stasis. Even as an instant must not push nor an atom press, creating motion where there was none, so a circle must not hesitate in circumference, creating stasis where pure movement was before.

The final stanza maintains anew how precarious is the balance, how anything "may jolt the Hand/That adjusts the Hair." Till that time, however, the hand does control the hair, even as consciousness can suspend the breath. If "our duty is to keep a delicate balance upon the hair of crisis," for "only by tempting death are we put in touch with divinity," as Weisbuch comments,[8] then this poem teaches us that although crisis may be the most extreme danger, the self has resources as well as obligations both to experience and to control it.

Peril becomes a possession, consequently, through the mind's ability to encounter, sustain, and comprehend extreme pain. Writing is a major part of the enterprise. For if consciousness keeps crisis balanced in a poise of clarity and pain for as long as possible, so the poem's precise measurement of the poise itself teaches the poet laws that govern its occurrence.

In her poems on pain, Dickinson defines its qualities, the range of its risks, and the scope of its rewards by charting its position in the various spaces of the mind. Although she may not be able to control its causes—those events in the external world which produce pain— she can in this way take control of its activity in her own mind, utilizing its very danger to arrive at insight.

2

Despair is the most extreme form of pain; consequently, the hardest to measure and the most in need of measurement. Although Dickinson devotes a large proportion of her poems to the analysis of pain in all of its varieties, a large proportion of her poems on pain are concerned in particular with despair.

Some poems about despair find perspective in contrast, like "The difference between Despair/and Fear." They surround this most special version of pain by defining other pains: where the differences are, there is despair. The poems that try to confront despair directly also seek out perspectives, using analogies to compare this mental state with other experiences from the external world, circling the hole that is despair until, in the process, its outlines emerge. Poems about despair directly are the most exploratory in form. They start out with questions, and the poems themselves, through their strategies of rhetoric, reach answers.

An essential difference between despair and lesser degrees or kinds of pain is the presence in the latter of fear, as poems like "The difference between Despair / And Fear" demonstrate. Fear, because it focuses upon a future situation, has a corollary within its own perimeters, which is hope. "When I hoped I feared – / Since I hoped I dared," begins poem 1181, neatly conjoining hoping, fearing, and daring to begin a poem about the power of a fourth and related action, suffering. "He deposes Doom / Who hath suffered him –," it rather smugly concludes. The following poem picks up the same cards to deal out a similar hand.

> Somewhat, to hope for,
> Be it ne'er so far
> Is Capital against Despair –
>
> Somewhat, to suffer,
> Be it ne'er so keen –
> If terminable, may be borne.
>   [1041]

Parallel construction links *hope* and *suffer,* implying that the awareness of a future tense makes any present endurable, because it must by definition give way at some point to something else, i.e., the future. The opposite is also implied: that in despair, against which hope is "Capital," time has been annihilated. There is no future, therefore no hope; therefore no fear.

Because it is timeless, because it is total—center and periphery—despair is "contented." Dickinson uses "contented" twice to describe despair. In "The difference between Despair / And Fear," the mind is contented as "the Eye / Upon the Forehead of a Bust – / That knows –it cannot see –," and in an even more astonishing analogy, poem 756 describes "A perfect – paralyzing Bliss – / Contented as Despair –."

> One Blessing had I than the rest
> So larger to my Eyes

That I stopped gauging – satisfied –
For this enchanted size –

It was the limit of my Dream –
The focus of my Prayer –
A perfect – paralyzing Bliss –
Contented as Despair –

I knew no more of Want – or Cold –
Phantasms both became
For this new Value in the Soul –
Supremest Earthly Sum –

The Heaven below the Heaven above –
Obscured with ruddier Blue –
Life's Latitudes leant over – full –
The Judgment perished – too –

Why Bliss so scantily disburse –
Why Paradise defer –
Why Floods be served to Us – in Bowls –
I speculate no more –

[756]

Although this poem seems more properly to belong in the next chapter, which is devoted to extreme happiness, or delight, the union it forms between bliss and despair tells us something not only about despair but about ultimate emotional states and their relationship to one another. "I stopped gauging – satisfied," Dickinson writes, a crucial line indicating both the hypothetical nature of the situation that the poem is so very busy measuring—gauging, and also another important danger inherent in ultimates, another way in which they interfere with as well as inspire the business of living. They annihilate the impulse to measure.

A spatial vocabulary runs rampant in every direction and dimension: "So larger," "this enchanted size," "the limit of my Dream" "The focus of my Prayer," "Supremest Earthly Sum," "Life's Latitudes leant over – full –," "The Judgment perished – too –." A blessing, a bliss is being described. Its dimensions are more than immense: they are periphery, *limit,* and center, *focus;* they are in the superlative degree— *Supremest.* Such totality creates perfection, or heaven on earth: no more want, no more cold; an "Earthly Sum" which veils by its nearer presence the distant future that is "heaven above." "Ruddier blue," a vivid oxymoron, means that the vitality (the pumping blood) of living color, primary color, earthly color, is closer and realer than an hy-

pothetical future. The geographical perimeters of earth (lati
close off this life from heaven; they make life full enough and wide
enough just as it is. There is no longer any need for a life beyond this
one, so that the Last Judgment becomes a purposeless concern.

Dickinson's vision of heaven on earth is as temporal as it is spatial.
As the bliss fills up all space, so it fills up all time. There is nothing
beyond it, neither distance nor future. And this is why bliss, perfect, is
also "paralyzing" – "Contented as Despair." Both are equally enervat-
ing, death-like states. Satisfied, you stop measuring. The mind is frozen in place when it can no longer push beyond itself towards
possibility, towards change, towards knowledge. Thus in her final
stanza, commenting upon her fantasy of perfect bliss, she tellingly
reverses and diminishes her earlier vocabulary of spatial and temporal enormity: "Why Bliss so *scantily* disburse – / Why Paradise
defer – " (my emphasis). Changing the proportions of the poem, she
offers us instead floods served "in Bowls." Suffering writ large, pleasure small: this situation, things as they really are, is revealed as necessary in order that one be able to "speculate" rather than to "speculate
no more." Its final words underline the insight that the entire poem as
a speculation, an exercise of the imagination, has granted its speaker.
The speculative act of poetry is good for measuring emotional states
that have occurred, and it is also useful for imagining situations that
have not happened elsewhere, such as perfect bliss, which turns out to
be paralyzing. In its process the poem reveals how the equivalent
perfection of despair—its ultimate and overwhelming totality, its
dreadful "contentment"—must be fought with precisely those
weapons that despair is so adept at destroying: the ability to gauge.

Poems attempting to confront despair directly reveal in their very
strategies of rhetoric both the difficulty of measurement and the need
for it.

> It was not Death, for I stood up,
> And all the Dead, lie down –
> It was not Night, for all the Bells
> Put out their Tongues, for Noon.
>
> It was not Frost, for on my Flesh
> I felt Siroccos – crawl –
> Nor Fire – for just my Marble feet
> Could keep a Chancel, cool –
>
> And yet, it tasted, like them all,
> The Figures I have seen

Set orderly, for Burial,
Reminded me, of mine –

As if my life were shaven,
And fitted to a frame,
And could not breathe without a key,
And 'twas like Midnight, some –

When everything that ticked – has stopped –
And Space stares all around –
Or Grisly frosts – first Autumn morns,
Repeal the Beating Ground –

But most, like Chaos – Stopless – cool –
Without a Chance, or Spar –
Or even a Report of Land –
To justify – Despair.

[510]

Writing of "Dickinson's two most crucial subjects, despair and death" (and, in particular, of this poem), Sharon Cameron observes that they "flood conception, overwhelm it, so that it gives way to tenuous, incomplete, and multiple representation."[9] Certainly Dickinson's technique in this brilliantly laborious attempt to "gauge" and hence possess despair is to surround its powerful and amorphous shape with other forms that are initially clearer, also less frightening. Only after thus creating an outline of her subject through the practice of circumference can she name it with her final word, "Despair." Although multiple representation is at the heart of this procedure, upon close analysis the poem appears neither tenuous nor incomplete.

The poem begins by testing the possibilities of negative reference. "The power of these negatives," writes Cameron, "is revealed in how firmly they stake out the territory of the known until all that is left is the vague and terrifying inference that this state is worse than physical death because, having most of its attributes, it is denied any of its reliefs: outside of time, it does not end."[10] This series of negatives simultaneously evokes and dismisses states that are themselves contradictory, so that differences are shown to permeate all potential similarities.

The first analogy is the most likely: death. We know how often Dickinson sees a connection between despair and "corporeal cost." But here, immediately, she has to reject the obvious similarities, "for I stood up, / And all the Dead, lie down –." Each negative proposal that follows in the first two stanzas likewise provokes, by contrast, an accompanying positive. The contrasts bring out difference without entirely destroying the initial awareness of similarity.

Seeking further analogies from the world of nature, the speaker invokes its time cycles, its seasons, its elements. Not night, for it is noon. Her image for noon is not one of color but of sound; not light in contrast to dark, but noise in contrast to stillness. For noon, the clanging of bells, bold and brazen with life, as indicated by the personification of bells putting out their tongues. The violence present in this image, intensified as the poem progresses, makes noon not exactly a happy contrast to dreary night; shows, in fact, ways in which night and noon may have something in common.

Again, in the following stanza, when frost is proposed and denied as a representation of the experience, because "on my Flesh / I felt Siroccos – crawl –," the choice of metaphor for depicting the feel of warm winds as contrasted to cold, *crawl*, is chilling. Immediately, however, the speaker denies the heat to which she has just attested—"Nor fire"—and then tries to describe a condition like cold that recalls her earlier association to death. Just her "Marble feet" alone (and their graveyard connotations) would cool the chancel of a church (this image, too, evoking funeral services—a suggestion immediately put into play in the next stanza).

This rapid succession of denials and assertions, in which images drawn from the natural world have been invoked to help characterize an unidentified mental state, has revealed a condition like death although it is life, like night although it is day, like cold although it is warm, like heat although it is cold. But analogies to the outer world are not identifications with it. Comparison must be complicated, even exploded, to measure properly.

Looking back upon her confusion of "no's" and "yes's," the speaker acknowledges both her impulse to make identifications and their analogical status: "And yet, it tasted, like them all." The word *taste*, introducing yet another sense perception (so far sight, sound, and touch have been included in the poem), indicates how emotional and sensory is the experience in question, which is why it requires the perspective of language to be explained.

In stanza three a new series of analogies begins, more developed than the earlier images. The growing verbal complexity of these descriptions is what accomplishes the surrounding and defining of the subject, "it." The first of these comparisons returns once again to death, recalling stanza one's "And all the Dead, lie down" as well as the "Marble feet" and chancel of stanza two, as it observes that "The Figures I have seen / Set orderly, for Burial, / Reminded me, of mine." A sense of death-in-life pervades, controlling the more specific images that follow. These four analogies are all in some degree in apposition to the figures set for burial, explaining how, why they remind her of herself. (At the same time, each analogy in the poem also parallels the opening word, "it.")

Now the metaphors become extreme, extraordinary. Dickinson is reaching beyond traditional associations with both the particularity and the juxtaposition of her figures, using the creative power of figurative language to find new combinations of words to say what she knows. A life "shaven," fitted to a frame," unable to breathe "without a key": images that show a self rigidified, reduced, imprisoned.[11] Each of my words of description strains at approximating Dickinson's figures for death-in-life, in their inadequacy demonstrating a central quality of metaphor, its resistance to paraphrase.[12]

Quickly, another analogy is produced, returning to and amplifying one of the speaker's original associations, the "Night" of line three. "It" is something like midnight, if midnight can stand for an experience "When everything that ticked – has stopped –," when "Space stares all around –." The ticking may be the life rhythms of the universe, or it may be the life pulse of the individual, even as the personification of space staring vacantly suggests an equivalent vacancy in the mind. So, in the next image, which returns to the frost of line five to describe how "Grisly frosts" on early autumn mornings "Repeal the Beating Ground," words about nature seem to describe an internal rather than an external event. The "beating" of the ground suggests more immediately an individual heart than throbbing vital forces in the earth, and the hint of personification in "grisly" helps to double the analogy back upon itself. In other words, the poem purports to describe an internal state, "it," by means of correspondences to the external world that, in their language, become more and more internal in reference. The clarification achieved by these later images, their success as opposed to the inadequacy of the poem's initial treatment of the same subjects, results from the way in which language now internalizes the external vocabulary that it has no better choice but to use. A dimensional vocabulary is needed to describe the space of the mind. Dickinson takes hers from nature (where else?) and, with metaphor, suits it to other purposes.

Although all of these analogies are drawn to death as subject and find a basis in it, none describe actual death. The life shaven is still able to breathe, albeit with a key; ticking has stopped but space is yet staring all around; the beating ground of autumn has been repealed by frost, not killed. This is not as much death as it is suspension of life, a state of the living mind so terrible because so like death; even more terrible, because unlike death it does not annihilate consciousness.

Dickinson's analogies define a circle that narrows as it curves. She admits to the developmental aspect of her process as she begins the final stanza: "But most, like Chaos –." Chaos is a spatial term not exactly taken from nature, referring as it does to the infinity of space of formless matter that preceded the existence of the ordered universe, to space that exists but is formless. Thus mental space and external space are no longer differentiated. Now the qualities with which the poem has been concerned throughout return again but in curiously suspended, abstracted forms: "Stopless"; "cool"; without a "Chance." We recognize in these phrases the endlessness of death, what happens when ticking stops and beating is totally repealed. We see once more the coldness of frost and marble, the hopelessness of the shaven life fitted to a frame, of space staring all around.

However, the poem does not end in this abstract mental space. To conclude her depiction of a state characterized by its disassociation from natural landmarks, Dickinson resorts to one more analogy, and a familiar one at that, linking chaos to a shipwreck: without "Spar – / Or even a Report of Land –." As it has proceeded, the poem has had to reject the buoys of the natural world (like death, frost, night, midnight) in its linguistic acknowledgment that they are, for all their similarities, not the mind. One of the horrors of this particular mental state is just that it is cut off from them, from everything. The analogies have revealed this. So the poem's final analogy is to a corresponding event in nature when one would, likewise, be cut off. On the other hand, total disconnection would mean, surely, a complete absence of language, that bridge suspended between mind and world. The condition of the speaker when she begins the poem is close to this. She cannot name what she feels, can say only "it." However, the closer she comes through the act of the poem to defining her condition, the less it is in fact one of complete isolation. The creating of an adequate language is what saves her, which may be why, although I have been insisting upon the importance of the way in which she shapes her language to mind space, at the same time, as in the final image, she never does forgo analogy, with its attempts to relate the natural world to the mind by including it in the poem.

The last line arrives at the name itself by tuning the definition of her condition more finely yet. One reading would deny that this is despair. In such chaos, where there is no evidence of land, this could not be despair; since, we could assume, despair is a human condition, and here in chaos we are beyond that. ("If the harried reader may be allowed one despairing quip, he may express his fear that the method itself as here employed is 'stopless.' For a final anticlimactic image of shipwreck is added . . . which fails even more to 'justify,' in the Miltonic sense, all this suffering," complains Anderson.[13]) Rather, I think that the final insight which at last allows Dickinson to name the condition is precisely that sense of being outside human time, human space, and human help. A report of land would, indeed, "justify" all this suffering; but then, with a purpose, the suffering would not be so bad. With no consciousness of anything beyond, it is this bad: it is *despair*.

The poem ends here, as it must, with the name. Because the word has been understood through a process of linguistic measurements that has surrounded it with concrete shapes and thereby revealed the most terrible of negative and formless mental experiences, despair.

In another poem of difficult definition, Dickinson's analogies turn into dramas with characters and settings to help her find the shape for the name, "Agony"; "Anguish."

> 'Twas like a Maelstrom, with a notch,
> That nearer, every Day,
> Kept narrowing its boiling Wheel
> Until the Agony
>
> Toyed coolly with the final inch
> Of your delirious Hem –
> And you dropt, lost,
> When something broke –
> And let you from a Dream –
>
> As if a Goblin with a Gauge –
> Kept measuring the Hours –

Until you felt your Second
Weigh, helpless, in his Paws—

And not a Sinew—stirred—could help,
And sense was setting numb—
When God—remembered—and the Fiend
Let go, then, Overcome—

As if your Sentence stood—pronounced—
And you were frozen led
From Dungeon's luxury of Doubt
To Gibbets, and the Dead—

And when the Film had stitched your eyes
A Creature gasped "Reprieve!"
Which Anguish was the utterest—then—
To perish, or to live?

[414]

Three analogues move rapidly from a felt correspondence between this mental state and nature to dramatic situations, "fictions," where metaphors more closely delineate the space of the mind.

The maelstrom is an image from the natural world, but as soon as it is equipped with a notch, as soon as it becomes a boiling wheel, then it is no longer some whirlpool off the coast of Norway but a force created exactly to reveal the mental event under consideration. This oncoming disaster, a torture of apprehension, is conceived of concretely, and yet in nearly the same breath it is identified as "the Agony," its concept. Conceived of, likewise, spatially, as you—the person experiencing—stands on something like a seashore, at the edge of this rising peril which approaches slowly, torturing her sense of growing terror with its deliberation. Spatially (the scene by the water's edge) yet also psychologically, as all concrete objects are personified: "the Agony/Toyed coolly"; "your delirious Hem." All manner of metaphors collide in a phrase like "delirious Hem" to evoke the mental space: synecdoche (the hem of the dress standing for the dress standing for the person standing for the mind of the person); personification (the hem feeling delirium, while the hem is standing for the edges of the person who is experiencing this frenzy); and a touch of hyperbole, even oxymoron, thrown in, too. All of this figurative reaching out from the bounds of the literal is necessary in order to stretch language into forms which are linguistic embodiments of the mental world.

This vocabulary is not only dimensional, it is dramatic: a scene is enacted. The person encountering the agony feels that she does drop into the maelstrom, is lost—and then is suddenly saved by an unknown force, so that the entire experience seems "a Dream." This dramatic fiction and the others that occur in the two following analogies calls attention to the narrative, active aspect of mental events which defines them as well as their dimensional matrix.

The poem continues with another complex analogy, also initiated with a comparison to a figure who belongs in the world's imagination, if not to the real world. But as the drama unfolds, this goblin, who represents "the Agony" of the first analogy, becomes Dickinson's own. In his "Paws" he has a "Gauge," with which he is holding and measuring the hours that belong to, synecdochically embodying, the protagonist: "Until you felt your Second / Weigh, helpless, in his Paws –." Perception of time, to translate, is helpless in the grip of this force; nor can the speaker's body come to the defense of her mind, so sensation of all kind is numbed. Again, the experienced torture is primarily due to consciousness of loss of control while in the grip of some powerful evil force: the fact that the self must watch its own passivity in the face of danger but cannot do anything about it. In this internal drama, even as the agony is personified and becomes a character, so some other agent, this time called God, comes to the rescue at the eleventh hour.

The third and final analogy portrays a prisoner, sentenced to execution, who is granted a last-minute reprieve. The linguistic leap from external back to internal world is accomplished by the description of the prison itself: "Dungeon's luxury of Doubt." The sudden introduction of the abstract vocabulary indicates that this is not a tangible dungeon but an imprisoned state of mind. The luxury of doubt is the possibility of hope, so that the move from dungeon "To Gibbets, and the Dead," is the one from fear to despair that I have discussed earlier. Finally, here as in the previous dramas, just as the speaker experiences what feels like the beginning of death ("when the Film has stitched your eyes" is an image of impotence similar to that of "the Eye / Upon the Forehead of a Bust – / That knows – it cannot see –"), she is reprieved. The third character who saves her is now labelled simply, "A Creature."

The question with which the poem concludes, "Which Anguish was the utterest – then – / To perish, or to live?", is something of a red herring, since it is not really the central question asked by the poem. But it does provide further information about what is the poem's central issue, the nature of the anguish under scrutiny. The question is rhetorical in that in each example the speaker obviously prefers to live—if only to be able to tell another tale, give another example. But the comparison made by the question is important, because again it identifies death as the nearest known counterpart to this psychological state. It labels them both as "utterest," and since death is the ultimate and final experience of the body, we understand this particular anguish or agony to be the ultimate mental pain. Although this poem does not specifically identify it as despair, the characteristics outlined here are familiar. A psychic coldness or numbness; powerlessness; timelessness; loss of control; consciousness of it all. To these are added torture. While dramatically represented as issuing from a diabolical other, that other, operating in the world of the mind that is the actual setting for the poem, is surely an aspect of self, one that seems as separate as it is evil. This sense of a divided self, of one as "Population" (1354) is the subject of many of Dickinson's poems, as I have observed in chapter 1: "Ourself behind ourself, concealed –/ Should startle most –" (670); "Of Consciousness, her awful Mate/The Soul cannot be rid" (894). In "It was not Death," despair is characterized as disassociation from nature; now it is further understood as internal disassociation, a self aware of separation within as well as without. Acute sensation of pain coupled with powerlessness to affect it; thus the self is both torturer and victim. This is "utterest" anguish, or despair.

If the differences and similarities between mind and world are always a central concern of consciousness (as I have pointed out in chapter 2), it is not surprising that these issues, heightened and strained to extremes (ultimates, utterests), become the axis upon which acute psychic experience is measured. In extreme pain the mind feels itself cut off from nature: "There is a pain – so utter/It swallows substance up –" (599); lost in the overwhelming totality of itself: "No Man can compass a Despair –" (477). Whereas in moments of power the mind gloats in this very isolation ("The Soul selects her own Society –/Then – shuts the Door –" [303]), the helplessness experienced in great pain turns disconnection into an additional component of the agony. This may be why, when language is used as a lifeline, it hooks quickly into the world of nature by means of analogy, in order to remedy the separation so acutely felt. But one to one correlations won't work: "It was not Death"—nor was it night, frost, fire, although it tasted like them all. It is when language, as it grows more sure of itself through the process of discrimination that analogy provides, more accurately represents the mind's condition with the transfers that metaphor enacts between concrete and abstract, dimension and idea so that it "doubles back" on its own suppositions, that the pain of separation is appeased. Language is connection; not because it makes the mind like the world (it doesn't), but because it turns the mind into the poem which is of the world.

In arguing for the exploratory and process-oriented nature of these poems about extreme pain, poems that measure in order to "possess," I am not suggesting that Dickinson wrote them in the act of undergoing despair, to save herself. She might have, but more likely they were written at some other time. However, the process of linguistic discovery that they reveal is an essential aspect of their structure and of what they say about emotional pain and how to deal with it. They show that the mind needs to make rhetorical tries upon its subject in order to name it, to bring it into language. Theirs is a rhetoric of circumference leading to control.

3

When Dickinson dramatizes mental anguish in "'Twas like a Maelstrom," she projects a plot with three characters. In my discussion of the poem I have concentrated thus far upon two of them: the impotent but alive conscious self and an evil, pain-dealing other. The third character is the savior—the one who brings release from pain. It, too, seems like an other, because the conscious self does not control it, either. Nevertheless, it can be no one but another aspect of self (Freud's superego?—one of her names for it is God). Whatever the basis for this division of self into three (Dickinson more customarily thinks in terms of two), the presence of the third character attests to one further attribute of mental pain: it can be overcome. Language may itself be an agent in the vanquishing of pain, although the insight and control that it produces need not necessarily diminish the pain. In "'Twas like a Maelstrom" the pain suddenly stops; in other poems it takes a long time to end. Writing of the ways in which pain lessens provides not only insight into yet another aspect of pain but one

further perspective from which to measure it. Poems in retrospect
have the advantage of distance that those which document the *media
res* cannot possess. Their rhetoric is, in consequence, less exploratory,
with time as a frame that encloses subject but also provides layers of
perception.

> It ceased to hurt me, though so slow
> I could not feel the Anguish go—
> But only knew by looking back—
> That something—had benumbed the Track—
>
> Nor when it altered, I could say,
> For I had worn it, every day,
> As constant as the Childish frock—
> I hung upon the Peg, at night.
>
> But not the Grief—that nestled close
> As needles—ladies softly press
> To Cushions Cheeks—
> To keep their place—
>
> Nor what consoled it, I could trace—
> Except, whereas 'twas Wilderness—
> It's better—almost Peace—

[584]

The domesticity of this poem's imagery is a clue to the difference
in perspective that is directly referred to here as "looking back." "Wilderness," a term used for the past state of anguish and grief in contrast to the present "almost Peace," is an apt description for the
various environments encountered in other poems like "It was not
Death" and "'Twas like a Maelstrom." Wild indeed are those places of
chaos, maelstrom, and gibbets, where space stares all around. But
from the vantage point of this poem's present, which is lack of anguish, the past of pain can be domesticated. The words used to describe it are drawn primarily from a vocabulary of dressmaking,
which seems the very opposite of wild.

Measurement and sewing are appropriate companions: what Dickinson is attempting to measure here is less sensation and more duration. "So slow / I could not feel the Anguish go," she observes as the
poem begins, then uses analogical process to ascertain more clearly
the nature of both staying and going.

Her first image parallels her last in that both are not domestic but
spatial. They set up the perspective, a sense of distance and dimen-

sion, within which the housebound activities of the second and third analogies are placed. The speaker is looking back on the "track" traversed by anguish. No longer a vivid artery of sensation, it has been "benumbed."

Consequently, she cannot say "when it altered": a word for change with connotations from the seamstress's vocabulary. Aptly, then, the first developed image of it, the anguish, is a dress, worn daily, nightly hung upon a peg. Like the "Childish frock" to which it is compared, anguish can be outgrown, but slowly, as the child grows, imperceptibly. ("As imperceptibly as Grief / The Summer lapsed away –," so Dickinson begins another poem, 1540, in which analogy's bridge between mind and world is built upon perception of this same trait.)

But this poem wants to make a more careful contrast between one kind of pain and another, between anguish and grief. The grief, it says in the third analogy, was more constant and closer to the skin. Not like a dress but an instrument used to make one, nestling close "As needles – ladies softly press / To Cushions Cheeks – / To keep their place –." The needles that ladies put into pincushions so as not to lose them. Domestic, yes; familiar, yes; but in their very domesticity and familiarity these images are also frightening. "Nestled," "softly press," "Cushions Cheeks": such phrases sound as if they are talking about cuddling a kitten, or a child. But their subject is the sharp needles of grief, even as the "Childish frock" is anguish. The perspective from beyond pain is more complex than that of calm after storm: it shows how long familiarity with pain makes its hurt in a perverse way comfortable and comforting.

Returning to her distance, to the present, the speaker concludes by looking again at the track, the space between past and present. Again unable to identify the cause of cessation, she can only concern herself with its nature as an environment: "Except, whereas 'twas Wilderness – / It's better – almost Peace –." Now we see how perspective compounds the meanings of these terms and of their contrast. Frocks and pincushions may seem more tame than wild, but Dickinson is pointing to a domestic savagery with its own kind of danger. Peace after pain may seem preferable, and so it is, better, but it is also numb, without feeling. There is almost a wistfulness, a yearning in these lines, for the time when anguish and grief, so dear in their way, were present.

It is interesting to compare this poem to another written without the perspective of distance on the experience of anguish; one which, however, uses similar imagery—needles. The differences in structure and tone between the vantage points of distance and immersion are underscored.

> A Weight with Needles on the pounds –
> To push, and pierce, besides –
> That if the Flesh resist the Heft –
> The puncture – coolly tries –
>
> That not a pore be overlooked
> Of all this Compound Frame –
> As manifold for Anguish –
> As Species – be – for name –

[264]

This poem is so insistent upon capturing sensation that it does not identify its subject, the "Weight," as anguish until its final lines. It is therefore much closer in procedure to poems like "It was not Death" and "'Twas like a Maelstrom" in which the speaker is so caught up in the feeling that she must first describe it, measure it, before she knows its name. The intense physicality of her sensation is also represented, here as in the other two poems, by a vocabulary that belongs more properly, or more literally, to body than to mind. Here "Flesh" is being pushed and pierced by a "Weight with Needles on the pounds."

The needles of "It ceased to hurt me" are noteworthy for the strange comfort that their pain brings; these stand for torture both violent and fiendishly subtle: they "push and pierce, beside –." The poem continues in phrases sharp and vigorous as the needles themselves to graph the situation, showing how "Heft" and "puncture" work to bring hurt to every pore: if the weight doesn't get you, the jabs will. The "Weight with Needles on the pounds" is, the speaker concludes using the poem's first analogy, "As manifold for Anguish – / As Species – be – for name –." Even as the individuals (names) in a species are varied but have common characteristics or qualities, so the manifestations of anguish, all related, can be numerous. In a familiar maneuver, a description couched in a physical vocabulary drawn from the external world is shown to apply to the internal world. Here, the weight seems literal until the analogy, moving from concept to concept, reveals it to have been metaphor: a way to describe the acute sensations that such mental experience provides.

Comparing these two studies of needles, one is struck by the different kinds of violence projected—household versus jungle—and also by a comparable difference in poetic structure: closure versus openness.

That same numbness which disconcerts the speaker of "It ceased to hurt me" is more assiduously measured in one of Dickinson's most well-known poems.

> After great pain, a formal feeling comes—
> The Nerves sit ceremonious, like Tombs—
> The stiff Heart questions was it He, that bore,
> And Yesterday, or Centuries before?
>
> The Feet, mechanical, go round—
> Of Ground, or Air, or Ought—
> A Wooden way
> Regardless grown,
> A Quartz contentment, like a stone—
>
> This is the Hour of Lead—
> Remembered, if outlived,
> As Freezing persons, recollect the Snow—
> First—Chill—then Stupor—then the letting go—
>
> [341]

Lack of feeling is always fearful to Dickinson. She seeks and demands the opposite: feeling, sensation, perception—life. Her poems about pain show her distinguishing not only between kinds of feeling but between kinds of non-feeling. There is the dullness of satiety (1678), a satisfaction that, being perfect, is paralyzing (756). There is the contentment of despair (756, 305), occurring when pain gets too great, when sense is setting numb (414). There is the trance that covers over the abyss which utter pain creates (599), what benumbs the track (584): this happens "After great pain": it is a "formal feeling." Essentially, lack of feeling in whatever form is a symbolic form of death, which brings the ultimate end of feeling. "And then / I could not see to see—" concludes a poem in which Dickinson hypothesizes the experiences of death ("I heard a Fly buzz—when I died—" 465); "And Finished knowing—then—" is the final line of "I felt a Funeral, in my Brain" (280), a poem using death as a metaphor for madness. That Dickinson frequently creates analogies between literal and metaphoric deaths, working in both directions between tenor and vehicle, has often been observed: the basis for these comparisons lies in the lack of feeling involved.

Lack of feeling, or various forms of "death," occasions the metaphoric transfers which interweave in "After great pain" to measure the effect of pain on the mind and body and, in consequence, to tell us something about the nature of pain itself.

Crucial is the poem's structure of "analogical progression" (Weisbuch's term): that is, a movement typological rather than linear, since each analogy, set in apposition to a central idea, proceeds only in that it further defines. Here a series of analogies for the "formal feeling" which comes after great pain call upon a range of external situations, intricately interrelated by metaphor. The feeling is internal, mental, but Dickinson uses words associated with the body, with nature, with society, and with physical death, as well with the mind, to shape and articulate both its sensation and significance.

First Dickinson outlines the feeling by describing the body's manifestation of it: nerves, heart, feet. In each instance, however, figurative language expands the experiential nexus. The nerves are personified; they "sit ceremonious." A social definition of formal—marked by form or ceremony—is called into play; the image may evoke a scene of ladies at tea. However, immediately they are compared to tombs. Formal meaning stiff or rigid; formal marking another kind of ceremony—that of death; more definitions are added. Now all ceremonies are suspect. And that is the point. Formal behavior, because it relies on predetermined patterns, because it proceeds by rote, is mindless.

Next we see the heart. It is stiff. Stiff is another definition for formal, here specifically denoting lack of feeling; for the heart can no longer tell how much time has elapsed between its present condition and when the great pain occurred: "Yesterday, or Centuries before?"

Then the feet. They move mechanically: formal meaning highly organized, also stiff, also devoid of thought, moving by rote—a kind of death. Their path, be it "Of Ground, or Air, or Ought," is wooden and regardless. Both nouns and objects describing the route of the feet, in their juxtaposition of concrete and abstract, indicate that this path is as conceptual as it is physical, and that the feet, like nerves and heart, function synecdochically for the person—especially, for the person's mind. *Ought* is a path taken by the mind: that of duty—a formal gesture. The conjunction of *Wooden* and *regardless* gives dimension to thought—or rather, to the lack of it. A final metaphor and analogy complete the stanza. "A Quartz contentment, like a stone," further describes the wooden way, but it is as well in apposition to "a formal feeling," like all of the images thus far. *Contentment* follows from *regardless* and *Ought,* while *Quartz* parallels *Wooden* and *mechanical;* each harkens back to *stiff, ceremonious,* and *Tombs;* all are aspects of *formal.* In the phrase "Quartz contentment" the concrete and abstract vocabularies are dramatically joined: two versions of rigidity, of formality, inform one another. The quartz is stiff and symmetrical—shaped in a formal pattern. With *regardless, Ought,* and *mechanical* to precede *contentment,* we recognize in that seemingly benign term the kind of formality with which the poem has been dealing throughout: the death-like impotence that marks it in other poems as a primary symptom of despair. We recall "A perfect – paralyzing Bliss – / Contented as Despair –," and the stone eye "that knows – it cannot see." The concluding analogy, "like a stone," comes as no surprise. A quartz contentment is a stony contentment, but the introduction of the word *stone* more directly yokes *Tombs* and consequently death to the image.

A formal feeling, then, is stiff, rigid, cold, conforming to patterns with no thought producing them, contented because of the absence of awareness, vitality, sensation, life. "Formal feeling" is really an oxymoron, for the feeling of no feeling.

The last stanza is introduced by a summarizing metaphor—"This is the Hour of Lead"—summarizing in that *Hour* and *Lead* hook on to the chain of epithets that have been defining formal in an increasingly ominous way. *Lead* is as heavy, dark, solid and inanimate as tomb-like nerves, stiff hearts, mechanical feet, wooden ways, and quartz contentment. *Hour* is the present tense of a mind that questions its understanding of time, that proceeds by rote, according to ought rather than insight, that has grown in its contentment, regardless. The "Hour of Lead" equals "a formal feeling": with its successive parallelism the poem comes full circle here, for the circle has outlined meaning.

But the poem is not over yet, because for all of the lack of a sense of time that accompanies the formal feeling, the poem, like "It ceased to hurt me," is concerned with temporal progression, from pain to the formal feeling to whatever succeeds it. Its first word is "After"; its concluding lines return from the stasis of the formal feeling to the process in which it is located. As the poem begins by setting out the past—what precedes the action of the poem—so its final analogy projects the poem into the future, what will hopefully (unless the formal feeling is truly death-dealing) follow: "Remembered, if outlived, / As Freezing persons, recollect the Snow – / First – Chill – then Stupor – then the letting go –." In this poem, too, time is a frame that holds the subject in place, through which one can study it.

Sharon Cameron's reading of these lines is excellent, noting as it does how the images themselves embody the temporal progression described.

> The image with which the poem concludes . . . is more complex because of its susceptibility to transformation, its capacity to exist as ice, snow, and finally as the melting that reduces these crystals to water. The poem's last line is an undoing of the spell of stasis. Because it is not another, different expression of hardness but implies a definite progression away from it by retracing the steps that comprise its history, we know that the "letting go –" is not a letting go of life, is not death, but is rather the more colloquial "letting go" of feeling, an unleashing of the ability to experience it again. To connect the stages of the analogy to the stages of the poem: "Chill –" precedes the poem, "Stupor –" preoccupies it, and "the letting go –" exists on the far side of its ending.[14]

In "After great pain," a dazzling demonstration of her analogical method, Dickinson is like a juggler: the balls she suspends in air so that their shapes and colors enrich one another to create the meaning of the whole are versions of "formal," taken from all manner of experiences in the world beyond the mind. The shape that they make as they circle in the air becomes, however, that of a mental experience: lack of feeling, a formal feeling. This poem is Dickinson's most intense and most precise definition of a condition that appears throughout her poetry on mental experience. This particular version of formal feeling comes after great pain; it is the self-protective response of the mind to a severe internal wound (it is the trance of "There is a pain – so utter –"), but it can prove dangerous in its own right. However, as I have pointed out, as a danger it dogs the complete experience of pain. It can precede, accompany, or follow pain. It is always a possibility, and it is more fearful than pain itself, because it is closer to death. One courts pain—hallows it—to escape this condition. However, even as opposites are in some ways nearer to one another than the gradations in between, so lack of feeling can swiftly succeed intensest feeling. To counteract its presence, one needs a "letting go"—an unleashing, in Cameron's words, of intensest feeling, again.

The pendulum of experience that Dickinson rides moves swiftly from intensest feeling to death of feeling and back again. She is not interested in the grey areas between. Her poems which describe the aftermath of pain show this by revealing from the perspective of distance the need for pain, even as do the poems describing the conditions that preceded pain: "Danger disintegrates Satiety / There's Basis there." The wistful yearning of "It ceased to hurt me" as well as the leaden impotence of "After great pain" both demonstrate this need.

The need for intense emotion. That emotion, for Dickinson, is usually pain of one sort or another. Delight—bliss—is, however, also emotion at the ultimate, but it brings its own difficulties, as the chapter to follow will describe. Already we have seen one of them—the fact that perfect bliss is paralyzing, thus contented as despair. Too much happiness leads to the same loss of feeling or psychic death as does too much pain—perhaps more readily and with more devastating results, as I shall show. On the other hand, a companion poem to "One Blessing had I than the rest" explains how delight can also serve as antidote to the formal feeling, providing impetus for the necessary "letting go."

> Did Our Best Moment last—
> 'Twould supersede the Heaven—
> A few—and they by Risk—procure—
> So this Sort—are not given—
>
> Except as stimulants—in
> Cases of Despair—
> Or Stupor—The Reverse—
> These Heavenly Moments are—
>
> A Grant of the Divine—
> That Certain as it Comes—
> Withdraws—and leaves the dazzled Soul
> In her unfurnished Rooms
>
> [393]

Delight, "Our Best Moment," is temporary. It has to be, or else it becomes the ultimate danger. The first stanza of this poem reaffirms the message of "One Blessing had I than the rest": if it *lasted,* it would "supersede the Heaven." But in the second stanza a medical metaphor is introduced to explain the useful properties which delight does, nevertheless, possess. Even as danger, in "I lived on Dread," is a stimulus or spur upon the soul, so delight, "Heavenly Moments," can be used as a reserve of emergency first-aid for what we have learned to identify as the most deadly psychic illness, "Cases of Despair –/ Or Stupor."

But one cannot live on it—as one can on dread. It is important to recognize, when discussing despair, the salutary properties of delight, but it is equally essential to be aware of its serious disadvantages. All told, danger is a safer medicine. There are less invidious side effects. For, as the third stanza underlines with its spatial metaphors of enclosure, of house and home, delight will have to be withdrawn, the "dazzled Soul" left in her "unfurnished Rooms." The sense of want becomes even greater when the desired object, possessed, has been taken away: the rooms appear, suddenly, unfurnished.

Better the want, however, than the gluttonous satisfied perfection of too much. Pain is a better source of stimulation, because it combines help with hurt in one dose. That is, it provides sensation, excitement, vitality, energy—all of which make one truly alive in the process as well as leading to knowledge, life's goal; but at the same time it causes suffering. Pain can't really be thought of as fun, because it hurts.

Dickinson's poems which surround and control pain achieve great insight into its nature. They show its attraction, as stimulus to the mind's intellectual and sensual appetites. It "Begets an awe / That searches Human Nature's creases / As clean as Fire." It is also "sweet": "Other impetus / Is numb – and Vitalless –." Sometimes it discloses "The Soul's distinct connection / With immortality." The poems show, too, its dangers, when pushed too far: "Corporeal cost" and also the living death of despair.

Measuring despair itself, Dickinson confronts headlong the most difficult and crucial dimension of pain. For despair is the turning point, where ultimate sensation becomes lack of sensation; where intense life becomes death-in-life. In this essay I do not deal with Dickinson's fascination with literal death: suffice to say that such concern finds its basis in the same investigation of life's extremes, a concern with what happens at the limits. Real death is one of those limits. Despair is another, in some ways more deadly, because during it consciousness does not cease but must watch, powerless to do anything but watch. Measuring is a major step beyond watching. To measure despair Dickinson has almost to invent language anew; certainly, she pushes figurative language to *its* limits in order to define and hence move the mind towards the control over its experience that had been missing, that had been a primary characteristic of the experience. Kinds of death serve as the analogical matrix for these poems that violently yoke and separate external and internal experience.

Finally, Dickinson gains insight into the nature of pain by viewing it from a distance. The perspective of afterwards, like the perspective of before, clarifies the desirability of pain: how it stimulates life, how its absence is yet another kind of death, how the formal feeling that follows pain, although its function may initially be therapeutic, in turn demands a jolt, a jar, some new stimulation (perhaps delight but more probably new pain) in order to keep the soul on its journey of exploration.

The language of poetry has measured all of this. It has encircled pain, studying it from the double perspectives of space and time, which become rhetorical strategies that can shape the outline of the subject at the center. Dickinson's parallel structures, her analogies complicated and exploded by metaphor, create a linguistic pattern of lateral rather than linear definition: hence my metaphors of circle, net, and juggler's balls. Comparisons proceed outward to explain a center; so Dickinson defines pain by comparing it with other emotions, with other conditions of body and world, with other periods of time before or after its presence, showing *is* through *like* and *unlike*. Poems that frame pain with time are more orderly, like a photograph; the poems which confront pain directly, *in media res,* rely heavily on dimension to give them some kind of perspective but nevertheless are more exploratory, more committed to process, in form and rhetoric.

Dickinson's analysis of pain at such a level of thoroughness and competence reveals a great deal about the way in which her poetry and her life were so entirely aspects of one another. She "hallowed" pain in order to achieve knowledge; she wrote about it in order to achieve power. The experience of pain that her poems document show it to be exciting, invigorating, demanding, dangerous, profound, and fruitful. Most important, however, about Dickinson's pain is that it is mental pain. Pain as Dickinson structures it for herself, by removing its autobiographical causes and connections to the social world, becomes entirely personal, completely private. This is pain for a world of one. The self who suffers and the self who measures are the same. But it is precisely because Dickinson knew how to confine her experience in significant ways that she could allow it to expand in others, ways in which she could be in control, so that peril might be possessed.

IV *"Delight is as the Flight"*

DELIGHT IS MORE DIFFICULT than pain for Dickinson to possess. Delight is more evasive, for it is more transitory: "Did our Best Moment
last . . ." It doesn't. Thus an interest in delight exposes one to another
kind of pain: loss. Also, delight is more dangerous than pain. It produces a "contentment" that can be "paralyzing": "I stopped gauging—
satisfied—" (756). In fact, delight's contentment involves another kind
of loss—loss of the self that Dickinson is at all times so anxious to
develop and maintain. Consequently, both possession and lack of it
are problematic where delight is concerned. Yet delight is under-
standably attractive to Dickinson. Intense and ultimate emotional experience, its place is opposite pain on the axis of extreme emotion.

Because she both wants delight and is afraid of it, Dickinson
develops several strategies for encountering it. Her poems view delight from the perspective of before (defining it as a concept, a potential situation), of *media res* (as it is happening), and of afterwards
(having had the experience). They work at controlling delight, not by
circling, trapping, to that extent taming it with words, as is her procedure with pain, but by relocating it in space and time, thereby
redefining its form and its meaning.

Poems from the perspective of before take a position that is fundamentally negative and reactive. Through compound analysis of its
nature, these poems try to ward off its effects—essentially by arguing
against the pursuit of delight. The dimensional vocabulary, the presentation of emotion as an event situated in mental space and time, is

put to the service of comparative relation: between wanting and having, having and losing, presence and absence, present and future, delight and loss. These poems of definition are abstract in tone and form. As a group, they comprise an elaborate and extremely rational system of defense—against something so very prized, so very feared.

Yet poems written *in media res,* from within the experience of delight, take another stance, with a different tone, style, attitude. Urgent and dramatic, they have a speaker who is an individual personality rather than an impersonal persona. These poems celebrate delight. In doing so, they bring the full weight of an hyperbolic rhetoric upon the goal of perpetuating delight, that it might never end. The poems from *media res* counter the cool rationality of the poems of definition with a language that unleashes the power of the imagination, of fantasy, to create a timeless state of pleasure. But this condition is highly volatile: as often as Dickinson can maintain fantasy with the structures of rhetoric, there are other moments when the prism is shattered, sometimes within the selfsame poem.

Finally, there are poems written from the perspective of after. Delight has been experienced. These poems offer a strategy that looks like a return to the negation in the poems of definition but is not. This is renunciation. Active rather than passive, it yokes reason with the imagination to create a mode of perception that uses the poem to reorder time and space so delight can occur without loss. This approach is also based upon the principle of ratio, because delight is always a relative situation. Renunciation puts memory and will at the service of sacrifice, makes of sacrifice a conceptual instrument that can reorganize the location of temporal and social conditions.

1

Delight's position in space and time is always at the center of any discussion of its merits.

> Delight is as the flight –
> Or in the Ratio of it,
> As the Schools would say –
> The Rainbow's way –
> A Skein
> Flung colored, after Rain,
> Would suit as bright,

Except that flight
Were Aliment —

"If it would last"
I asked the East,
When that Bent Stripe
Struck up my childish
Firmament —
And I, for glee,
Took Rainbows, as the common way,
And empty Skies
The Eccentricity —

And so with Lives —
And so with Butterflies —
Seen magic — through the fright
That they will cheat the sight —
And Dower latitudes far on —
Some sudden morn —
Our portion — in the fashion —
Done —

                    [257]

Ratio is identified in the first stanza as the principle of measurement most appropriate for delight, although Dickinson hastily
finds a concrete example to substitute for this bookish abstraction.
The "Rainbow's way" is an image from nature that calls attention to
the spatial configuration of the situation as well as its beauty. But in
the poem's opening line there is yet another equivalent for ratio, for
the "Rainbow's way," and for delight that shows the connection between all three: it is "the flight." The first line of the poem is a tidy
Dickinson aphorism and analogy in one succinct phrase: "Delight is as
the flight —." Flight equals "in the Ratio of it," because its movement
creates a relationship between one place (here) and another (there).
The motion is characterized, however, by a specific direction: away.
Something present going, implying a future, a "gone." Ratio has to do
with the relationship between present and future as much as between
here and there: a temporal situation is construed spatially, envisioned
as "The Rainbow's way."

In the second half of the first stanza Dickinson elaborates upon
the significance of her analogy, upon the connection between flight
and delight, what makes them "rhyme." Brightness is not all: the
rainbow image suits her meaning not simply because it is gaily col-

ored, but because it is ephemeral. The "Skein/Flung colored, after Rain," like a rainbow, like delight, in color and form is not the right metaphor because it is too solid. The fact of flight contributes to this sort of nourishment: the fact of impermanence, which is rareness, too.

Understanding of the necessity of flight to rainbows is a pragmatic awareness, tinged with the bitterness of experience. This is the theme of the second stanza, but its opening wish, " 'If it would last,' " presents in the subjunctive mood the other side of the matter, the desire for permanence that is equally central to Dickinson's difficulties with delight. Even as she understands how its transitory nature is a part of delight's delightfulness, she wishes it were not so. Here, she associates the "unrealistic" desire for permanence with childhood (in poems where she creates delight as timeless she often speaks with the persona of a little girl); in fact, it is a need she never does "outgrow." Here she pictures herself as a child naively taking rainbows "as the common way," calling "empty Skies/The Eccentricity." Thinking that beauty and "glee" are rule, not exception.

The final stanza reminds us of the analogical function of her rainbow image: "And so with Lives –/And so with Butterflies –." That is, and so with the role of butterflies in lives, since butterflies, like rainbows, are good symbols for delight, with their bright beauty and ephemeral nature—their flight. The stanza also intensifies the nature of delight's components. Its beauty and excitement become "magic," while the inevitable loss of their presence becomes "fright" (another rhyme for delight). Here are the two edges of the sword that is delight. Magic, to paraphrase the cryptic phrasing of these final lines, can be seen only through the fear that it will go, vanish, "cheat the sight." Dickinson's description of magic's flight is emphatically spatial, granting form and shape to the "school's" concept of ratio. Fright is a frame through which the magic is viewed, so that delight is surrounded by a perspective of pain. Fright, painful enough in itself, looks to a future of greater pain, when the butterflies, the magic, will "Dower latitudes far on –/Some sudden morn –." *Latitudes, far, sudden, morn* give to loss both spatial and temporal dimension, emphasized by the final two lines and especially by the final word, "Done –." Flights may begin here, but they end there: out of sight. The ratio that must be measured and understood is the proportion between having and losing, presence and absence. Obviously, if rainbows are the eccentricity, empty skies the common way, this proportion is weighted in favor of pain.

The ratios that exist when delight is concerned indicate relation between spaces; another poem defines delight by making explicit the frame structure implicit in "Seen magic – through the fright."

> Delight – becomes pictorial –
> When viewed through Pain –
> More fair – because impossible
> That any gain –
>
> The Mountain – at a given distance –
> In Amber – lies –
> Approached – the Amber flits – a little –
> And That's – the Skies –
>
> [572]

Pain is again the frame, the present environment, so that delight becomes a prospect viewed, a picture. It is delight's relationship to pain that makes it "pictorial": its distance gives it outline and separateness. As a picture, it is art (which makes pain life).

"Pictorial" is paralleled in the first stanza by "more fair." Another characteristic of art, therefore, is that its beauty exists in a comparative relation to something else. The nature of this relationship is explicated in the second stanza. The first stanza devotes its conclusion to explaining why a picture requires the comparative degree. The frame that sets delight apart seals it off, too. It therefore exists in another place and cannot be identified, only compared, with the here in relation to its there.

The poem parallels its first image of frame and picture with another, drawn from the world of nature, analogous in structure: a mountain framed in amber. From the perspective of distance a mountain appears both beautiful and inaccessible, as if encased in a protective hard shell. The quality of the light is what creates the frame: the color of amber, which skies also share, generates, because viewed from a distance, an image of amber's physical properties as well. But if the first two lines of the second stanza parallel with their concrete vocabulary the first two lines of stanza one, so that delight and mountain are analogous, pain and amber, the second stanza's final two lines contrast with rather than modify their counterparts in stanza one.

They alter the perspective, remove the frame, and show what happens when there is a shift in the proportions of the experience. From close up, what seems as hard as amber moves; becomes "the Skies." Now the viewer shares the same environment with the mountain, the skies, so that the delight that the mountain embodies is no longer pictorial, a world apart. Fair, perhaps, but not more fair. Life, and no longer art. Its very proximity makes the mountain different because no longer impossible to approach. In other words, frames help make pictures pictorial, and special, by separating them from the viewer's present reality. Remove the frame, turn what looked like amber into skies, and the picture loses some of the qualities that have defined it as pictorial in the first place, have made it so desired.

The following poem provides a gloss upon the themes of "Delight – becomes pictorial –."

> Satisfaction – is the Agent
> Of Satiety –
> Want – a quiet Commissary
> For Infinity.
>
> To possess, is past the instant
> We achieve the Joy –
> Immortality contented
> Were Anomaly.
>   [1036]

This interplay among concepts is aphorism without images; rhyme serves to complicate the analogical pattern. Specifically, a single rhyme pattern links most of the key words in identity or contrast: "Satiety," "Commissary," "Infinity," "Joy," and "Anomaly." Two of the poem's central concepts, "Satiety" and "contented," are already familiar to this discussion: in the context of pain, however, not delight.

Personification in the first stanza provides a concrete element in the dense abstraction. Satisfaction and want are portrayed as agents, deputies for other concepts. When one experiences them, in other words, one gets a taste or an example of something more comprehensive. They visit the central self (hence the active nature of emotional experience is manifested). Satisfaction and want are placed in contrast to one another; consequently, the forces which they represent, satiety and infinity, are also opposites, though their polarity might be less immediately obvious. They may be viewed as standing at opposite ends of a spectrum (since they are also linked in a relationship by means of rhyme). Because want is infinity's representative, infinity becomes more than a space or distance; it is an emotional event, as well. It is the opposite of satiety: an endless state of wanting, not getting, and, consequently, expecting the ever-possible.

We have seen the word "Satiety" before. "Danger disintegrates Satiety," Dickinson declares in "Peril as a Possession": "There's Basis there." Satiety, when viewed as a state of emotional lethargy and inactivity, is an old enemy. It generally causes, as it does in the second stanza of this poem, contentment, another condition of which we have learned to be suspicious.

The second stanza, although it parallels the first, considers the problem in terms of actions rather than their implications. "To possess" parallels "Satisfaction" structurally; experientially, satisfaction results from possessing. But this chart of cause and effect places a new and delicate point on the satiety-infinity continuum: "the instant / We achieve the Joy." That moment has to be just a flicker, poised and then gone (we recall rainbows and butterflies), because feeling it cannot lead to possessing it without dire results. The final lines explain why, as they link joy with infinity and immortality (and contrast it to anomaly). Again, rhyme underscores these relationships. "Immortality contented" is a contradiction in terms—an oxymoron, an "Anomaly." Joy, like other of the poem's actors, is also an agent or commissary: for immortality (therefore closer to want than to satisfaction), even as immortality is a version of infinity. Contentment, perfect and paralyzing, has nothing to do with immortality, forever poised, itself the brink, of possibility. Contentment, possession, satiety, and satisfaction are all closer to the condition of despair than they are to joy or delight. Like "Delight—becomes pictorial—" and Dickinson's important simile, the perfect, paralyzing bliss "Contented as Despair," this poem shows how close to delight is active pain, how close to despair is inactive pleasure. All depends upon the ratio or proportion between the emotions being measured. Yet the poem also suggests that there is a place between delight framed by distance and delight possessed, a butterfly poise that is possible, perhaps.

In another poem that maneuvers with a similar vocabulary, Dickinson demonstrates how pleasure must be defined with pain within its boundaries.

Expectation – is Contentment
Gain – Satiety –
But Satiety – Conviction
Of Necessity

Of an Austere trait in Pleasure –
Good, without alarm
Is a too established Fortune –
Danger – deepens Sum –
                              [807]

Expectation, contentment, satisfaction, pleasure, danger—these
are the now recognizable landmarks in Dickinson's emotional terrain.
Again, what she wishes to do here is to locate them vis-à-vis one
another. This poem, like "Satisfaction – is the Agent," essentially abstract in vocabulary, relies on linguistic position—apposition and opposition—to establish psychological value.

Yet its first two lines are jarring, for now satiety and contentment
are opposites, not synonyms, just as expectation and gain are contrasted. How can expectation be contentment?

We need to ascertain the relative positioning of these emotional
concepts to understand the shift in Dickinson's new use of an important term. Even as expectation and gain are placed opposite one
another, so the equivalencies set up between expectation and contentment, gain and satiety means that the latter terms, contentment and
satiety, are in opposition. The similarity between gain and satiety is
simple: when you are fed, you get full. However, the opening equation is, and is meant to be, startling. "Expectation – is Contentment –"?
We need the rest of the poem to understand how wanting might make
one content.

Yet as the poem continues, it focuses upon satiety, further
defining it in its relationship to pleasure. The fact that this full feeling
will accompany pleasure is predictable enough, but that this very
fullness should therefore be indicative of an "Austere trait" in pleasure is not self-evident, since the severity, sternness, and solemnness
associated with "Austere" would seem closer to pain than to pleasure.

To this point in the poem Dickinson has been piling up abstractions with nary a verb or qualifying phrase between: *Expectation, Contentment, Gain, Satiety, Conviction, Necessity, Austere trait, Pleasure.* The
concepts are like cards being dealt into place on a table. They are
related by their position: the single copula, the two genitives, the one

preposition enforce associations that the dashes indicate. This rapid setting out of terms with their provocative assertions is followed, paralleled, and explained by a financial analogy. Money, too, has to do with measuring. The "fortune" that is "Good, without alarm" is, in its reliability and abundance, boring. Amassed, its very existence depletes energy rather than incites it. Thus it has its painful aspects, its "Austere" elements. Danger, on the other hand, "deepens Sum –" Uncertainty of possession, even pain, undergone in the process of acquisition, makes the coin more valuable. "Sum" is not fixed but can be deepened, because it involves psychological as well as monetary value. Therefore, the contentment of expectation is the satisfaction of knowing that one is in a state of unpredictability, excitement, danger, and possibility. The austerity of pleasure is its bleak and painful surfeit. Here, playing with her own vocabulary of emotional concepts, Dickinson makes "Austere" more like the "content" that we are used to, "Contentment" more like the "Basis" that "Disintegrates Society."

The purpose of this juggling with emotional commonplaces is to provide a more profound perspective on the nature of delight. Contrary to popular opinion, these poems assert with their logical, analytic format that encountering delight means encountering pain. In the following poem, the association between delight and despair is so close that they interpenetrate one another. However, they are not the same, which is why their connection is so powerful and so curious. If pain and delight were really one, the difficulty would not be as acute. It is because they interact profoundly with one another but are yet distinct, with different emotional and intellectual consequences, that Dickinson works so hard at measuring their relative positions.

> Delight's Despair at setting
> Is that Delight is less
> Than the sufficing Longing
> That so impoverish.
>
> Enchantment's Perihelion
> Mistaken oft has been
> For the Authentic orbit
> Of its Anterior Sun.
>   [1299]

The spatial configurations of the poem are those of circular trajectories: orbits upon which the location of bodies are charted. As the poem begins, we see the closest possible juxtaposition, the possessive construction linking despair to delight through ownership, through participation: "Delight's Despair." Personification makes the relationship more intimate yet. It is delight who feels despair, the feeling arising as delight, who is also a sun, sets—as every sun, in the natural order of things, must do. Delight's feeling of despair is further particularized as arising from the understanding that delight itself is "less" (in duration? intensity? significance? we don't know yet) than what succeeds delight's setting, a condition of longing that suffices as much as it impoverishes.

The aphoristic pronouncements of the first stanza are obscure enough that a second stanza in analogous relation is helpful. Here the planetary vocabulary makes overt the spatial nature of the problem.

Perihelion is that point of the orbit of a planet or comet which is nearest to the sun. Enchantment is thus the planet or comet, not the sun. The orbit of enchantment may, however, be mistaken for the other "Authentic" orbit of its sun.[1] The sun is delight, and it is, in the cosmography of this poem, the nearest celestial body to enchantment. And enchantment? The very proximity of their two orbits should tell us, for what shares that nearness to delight in stanza one is the longing that follows close upon the setting of delight. That lingering longing, because it at once satisfies and depletes, is the enchantment, not delight itself: the false sun of a parhelion, if Dickinson were conflating the two astronomical terms, or of the moon, which is another kind of false sun. Because delight is by its nature fleeting, and longing, by its nature, long, the latter has its own very real appeal, its semblance of delight. But though it has a moment in which it closely resembles delight, its path leads in a different direction, to despair, because it is always and ever longing, never gain. The orbits of the two bodies come closest together at the moment when delight ceases and longing, like the moon rising after the setting of the sun, begins anew. This is delight's despair.

Thus these poems show how delight and despair, albeit emotional opposites, inform one another. Even as there is a condition of delight's despair, there is also, described although not labelled by the following poem, despair's delight. Because delight is so ephemeral, Dickinson's analyses of it devote extensive time and concern to its absence, to what precedes and what follows it. Especially, as we have already seen in poems like "Satisfaction – is the Agent / Of Satiety –," "Expectation – is Contentment –" and "Delight's Despair at Setting,"

the necessity, value, delight of wanting—of a present tense lived in a
projected future—is central to the compound experience.

> Who never wanted – maddest Joy
> Remains to him unknown –
> The Banquet of Abstemiousness
> Defaces that of Wine –
>
> Within its reach, though yet ungrasped
> Desire's perfect Goal –
> No nearer – lest the Actual –
> Should disenthrall thy soul –
>
> [1430]

Not only may want be preferable to delight, it is a necessary
condition for delight's very existence. "Maddest Joy" does not happen
to someone who "never wanted." An analogy puts the situation in
terms of bodily, instead of emotional, fulfillment and denial. "The
Banquet of Abstemiousness" is a fruitful oxymoron. Its surfeit of self-
imposed nothingness makes a vivid contrast to the more usual image
of sensory indulgence, the banquet of wine. You can't have both,
aphoristically declares the speaker: pleasure unsought is marred, is
not really pleasure. Thus the first stanza asserts the need for need. It
may remind us of other of Dickinson's lines on this topic: that, for
example, "The Summit is not given / To Him who strives severe / At
middle of the Hill –" (772).

The second stanza makes the matter of want, of desire, even
more crucial. "Desire's perfect Goal" is the condition of Tantalus:
"Within its reach, though yet ungrasped." Some consider this to be
torture. Yet when Dickinson explains the price of possession, we see
what kinds of pain have to be considered here. For possession of "the
Actual" will "disenthrall thy soul –." An extreme statement, that one's
very soul should somehow be loosened, lost at the moment of getting
what one has sought. The line is doubly startling, both in its hyperbole
and also in its suddenness. The poem has not been talking of the soul
or its equilibrium; only, it seemed, the relationship between desire
and maddest joy. Yet when we consider the nature of this disenthrallment, we find a clue to its inclusion back in stanza one, in its brief
discussion of banqueting. Wine certainly represents, paralleling it,
"maddest Joy"—something desirable, delightful, rich, and tasty. Yet

wine is intoxicating, too. It gets you drunk, so that you "lose your senses." Its effects are not conducive to vigor, to discipline, to work. Even as, when we consider it more carefully, "maddest Joy" is as suspect as it is appealing. *Maddest?* Insanity is equivalent to drunkenness, both producing loss of control. On the other hand, wanting, reaching, desiring are themselves exciting and without harmful side-effects: "Desire's perfect Goal –."

This analogous relationship between maddest joy, the banquet of wine, and the soul's disenthrallment is examined more thoroughly in another poem, one to which I have had occasion to refer before. The context of "Power is only Pain" is an extended comparison between pain and delight.

> I can wade Grief –
> Whole Pools of it –
> I'm used to that –
> But the least push of Joy
> Breaks up my feet –
> And I tip – drunken –
> Let no Pebble – smile –
> 'Twas the New Liquor –
> That was all!
>
> Power is only Pain –
> Stranded, thro' Discipline,
> Till Weights – will hang –
> Give Balm – to Giants –
> And they'll wilt, like Men –
> Give Himmaleh –
> They'll Carry – Him!
> [252]

Liquids and solids regulate the poem's image patterns. Stanza one contrasts the water of grief with the wine of joy. There is, however, no abstinence here: grief comes in quantity, pools. Whereas a little joy goes a long way and is ultimately much more devastating in its effects. It overpowers the speaker, breaks up her feet; she tips, "drunken."

Which leads Dickinson to the matter of power, a concern at the heart of most of her researches. Here she identifies power with pain, because, by means of one's own discipline, one can possess it. By controlling it with "Weights," one can use it for her own purposes. Control is the key. Control is power. And, in this poem, at any rate, delight cannot be controlled.

Each stanza in the poem juxtaposes two contrasting images of pain and pleasure. In stanza one the speaker is in control of grief (she wades whole pools of it and never drowns), while "the least push of Joy" puts her out of control, intoxicates her. In stanza two the solid image of pain with weights hung upon it is set against an hyperbolic depiction of the effects of "Balm." As liquidness joins the images of the first stanza, here the controlling metaphor is solidity. The speaker's own discipline has turned the pools of grief into something so solid that weights will hang on it. In the contrasting image Dickinson shows the effects of liquid delight upon those mythic embodiments of strength, bulk, and power—giants. Just as the little human speaker tipped, drunken, in stanza one, so giants will wilt from the effects of balm in stanza two. Give balm to "Himmaleh," the personified god or spirit of the Himalayan Mountains (an image of massive force), and even he will be completely overwhelmed, overpowered, out of control: "They'll Carry – Him!"

Loss of control is the poison hidden in the velvet glove of delight. Fearful beyond measure. Pain can cause it, too; when it reaches the debilitating extreme that is despair. But delight is more dangerous, because it is attractive, seductive. It promises all that is beautiful and wonderful. One gets caught off guard before it, with defenses down.

Delight's propensity to intoxicate its possessor, to disenthrall her soul, confounds further the difficulties posed by delight in its rareness, by the fact that the total experience under consideration must be encountered as a problem in ratio between absence and presence. To engage in the business of happiness means to undergo the pain of having delight (with its loss of control), the pain of not having delight (first wanting, then losing).

"'If it would last'/ I asked the East." That wish, unexpressed for the most part, lies behind these poems upon the nature of delight, poems that can be viewed as an austere aesthetic for coping. Their assertion of the value of desire by itself, the harm of fulfillment, the necessity of loss, are a fierce attempt at self-education and self-discipline from a personality all too eager for the blandishments of delight. The poems represent genuine insight into the patterns and complexities of this psychological situation, but they are at the same time elaborate structures of defense.

Abstract and persistently theoretical, these poems are sealed off both from autobiography and even from much metaphorical activity. Analogies are usually present to provide a dimensional framework for the situations under analysis; however, the conceptual emphasis of their rhetoric is striking. Yet when we get a glimpse of the causes of delight, we understand more clearly the poetic and psychological strategies that the poems employ. When we look to another body of poems, those written *in media res,* with a speaker experiencing delight rather than evaluating it, we discover what we may have suspected from the first: that love is delight's most frequent cause. The following poem, however, although it belongs to the poems of definition, does identify a source for delight. Again the theme of flight and its association with delight is developed; again we see the close relationship that must exist between delight and pain. But here the cause, "Friends," provides a basis that makes ratio a concern more than mathematical.

> Are Friends Delight or Pain?
> Could Bounty but remain
> Riches were good –
>
> But if they only stay
> Ampler to fly away
> Riches are sad.
>
> [1199]

"Could Bounty but remain" ("'If it would last' / I asked the East"): one more ratio that organizes delight is the one between the perception of impermanence and the need for permanence. The relationship between delight and pain has to do with staying power.

It also involves an element in the formula not emphasized in other poems that we have studied: "Ampler." The rainbow finally experienced may be qualitatively different from the one anticipated. It may be better. If so, its loss is consequently greater. The comparative degree is crucial to the construct. A financial analogy once again provides clarification. Riches in the abstract are a matter of numbers; value—"good" or "sad"—derives from their relative position vis-à-vis the one possessing them. "Good" if they would stay; "sad" when they are lost, especially because presence has made them more valuable, more cherished. Position is temporal—before, during, after—and also qualitative. The answer to "Are Friends Delight or Pain?" depends entirely on one's relative position to the "Bounty" in question.

It is not better, for Dickinson, to have loved and lost. Better not to love at all, if delight is as the flight, if love must inevitably fly away, richer and therefore more painful because it has been known. There are certain pains that Dickinson may want to hallow, but there are others she will go to great lengths to protect herself from. The pain of loss is surely one of the latter. It is so powerful that fear of its presence informs the state that should be its absence, delight itself. Friends are delight *and* pain: "Seen magic–through the fright/That they will cheat the sight–/And Dower latitudes far on–/Some sudden morn–/Our portion–in the fashion–/Done–" (257)

Defining the nature of delight, Dickinson's careful measurement, her weighing of proportion in fine ratios of location, degree, effect, and significance, is a way to build structures of defense against delight's allure. Ratio is a tool of the intellect ("As the Schools would say"); Dickinson uses it to establish knowledge as need's opponent. The message collectively conveyed by these poems is firm; don't do it. And yet, at the same time as they denigrate it, they also reveal the need, the desire, the want. Ascribed to a less sophisticated, often childish aspect of the self, it is nonetheless the driving force behind all the energy that these poems discharge, all the work they do as agents of invalidation.

In their busy proportioning out of relative rewards and penalties, these poems do also acknowledge a butterfly poise: "the instant/We achieved the Joy–" (1036). That is knowledge as well as need. It turns out to be the chink in this austere armor. Other poems of hers find ways to turn that small hole, that fragile moment, that glimpse of rainbow, into a shower of gold which fills the sky.

2

Dickinson writes poems in which she is experiencing delight. Whereas her poems of definition are characterized by their precision of measurement, their analytic nature, those in which the speaker feels delight are urgent in tone, dramatic in structure. They rush, exclaim, invoke. Their purpose is less to define emotion than to release it through articulation. They have, as befits their dramatic form, a speaker with an individual rather than an impersonal persona, a personality whose exciting situation is the focus of the poem. And while poems from the center of pain use rhetoric to control and to contain violent emotion, poems where the speaker is caught up in delight seek to hold onto emotion, keep it going, perpetuate it through the intensity of a rhetoric that is essentially celebratory.

> Mine – by the Right of the White Election!
> Mine – by the Royal Seal!
> Mine – by the Sign in the Scarlet prison –
> Bars – cannot conceal!
>
> Mine – here – in Vision – and in Veto!
> Mine – by the Grave's Repeal –
> Titled – Confirmed –
> Delirious Charter!
> Mine – long as Ages steal!
>
> [528]

This poem contradicts outright Dickinson's warning that "To possess, is past the instant / We achieve the Joy –" (1036). The joy that this speaker experiences is entirely involved with possession, as the emphatic repetition of "Mine" attests. The poem is, in fact, a catalogue of symbols that mark the speaker's right to possession, while its tone is one of unmitigated delight. In this way the poem associates delight and possession as thoroughly as do the poems of analysis, which tend to bemoan the conjunction.

The first stanza lists three proofs of possession: "the Right of the White Election," "the Royal Seal," "the Sign in the Scarlet prison." Such images are at least in part responsible for the tone of the poem: "Exclamatory," "rapturous," "describing a state of extreme ecstasy," comments Charles Anderson, "the rhetoric of hymns." The vocabulary of covenant theology, says Karl Keller. The language is most certainly ritual, religious.[2]

Yet at the same time it is resoundingly legal. (Possession may be nine tenths of the law, but Dickinson is interested in affixing to her condition of ownership signs—and seals—that prove it to be so.)

These objects and events, election, seal, and sign, are literal but symbolic. "There" in no Amherst setting, they are, rather, "there" in a situation of imagination; they are symbolic embodiments of "Right."

One can seek out "meanings" for these images, but the pursuit is not particularly rewarding. "Election" is certainly consonant with Puritan achievement, but the royal seal bespeaks a different source of power, whereas the mysterious scarlet prison is not directly associated with either.[3] Commenting on Dickinson's use of the Puritan system, as stimulus rather than stricture, Keller finds her personal use of the vocabulary to be a familiar pattern: "religious imagery giving way to her expressiveness, herself given a voice by inward obligation."[4] Although their sources or symbolism may be elusive, these images are clearly ritual, mystical, and legal. They show that the speaker has been favored with signs of a most special grace. She is elect, she has royal permission, within a very prison she has been granted a sign.

The second stanza focuses upon a particular and important property of her ownership, again using a rhetoric which is essentially a catalogue of parallel images or examples of the same phenomenon. That property is irrevocability. If we remember those many poems of definition in which delight's greatest curse is its ephemerality, "the flight," in which possession becomes satiety, "a too established Fortune," we can understand that when Dickinson imagines the achievement of delight, she will have it on other terms: "If it would last." Hers, then, is a delight that is eternal ("by the Grave's Repeal," "long as Ages steal"), but at the same time, it is "here." *Vision* and *Veto* reveal again that combination of mysticism and legality which informs the poem. The power to see, the power to deny—these have been granted the speaker. To see the wonder of this experience, to deny its closure: thus I would interpret these enigmatic words. "Delirious Charter," exclaims the speaker about her right of possession, now titled and confirmed, her metonymy descriptive of her own state of mind rather than of the symbol of possession itself—delirious. (Dickinson's alternate phrase, "Good affidavit–," also manifests the importance of legal possession here.) The final simile, "long as Ages steal," is a final assertion of power, once more from a legal perspective. "Steal" means to pass or happen imperceptibly, gently, gradually; but it also means, of course, to take the property of others without permission. Thus, "Mine–long as Ages steal" means both for all eternity and also that though ages may try to steal the possession, the speaker is confident of her power to safeguard it, to keep it for herself.

The poem never identifies what or who is "Mine." Its focus is not external but internal; its concern is with what the speaker feels because she has what she wants. That feeling, as the exclamatory rhetoric reveals, is one of supreme happiness and pride—delight.

Dickinson's vision of achieved delight is of delight as she would have it be. Some experience in the external world may have given rise to the poem, but the poem is an articulated fantasy. Her possession of power marks a primary difference between this and her more "realistic" versions of the same situation, which condemn it for causing loss of power: "Give Himmaleh –/ They'll Carry – Him!" The accumulated symbols and signs, the seals and charters, are testimonies to her authority. (She needs so many, needs to repeat so persistently, perhaps because she must convince herself as well as her audience of her strength.) Once she feels secure, however, she can celebrate with intense enthusiasm her delight in possession, her possession of delight. The exclamation marks, the repetition, the strange symbols, all give to the poem a liturgical tone. The legal underpinnings of the language enhance its strength with worldly basis. Finally, our primary impression of the poem is of its tone, its delirious delight; form and vocabulary reveal something about how the speaker got that way.

Other poems *in media res* permit realistic undercurrents: their delight is, consequently, less unequivocal.

> Come slowly – Eden!
> Lips unused to Thee –
> Bashful – sip thy Jessamines –
> As the fainting Bee –
>
> Reaching late his flower,
> Round her chamber hums –
> Counts his nectars –
> Enters – and is lost in Balms.
> [211]

"Eden"—Paradise—is synonymous, as in many of Dickinson's poems, with happiness or delight. This is not the paradise of the soul after death, however, but an incarnation of the first Eden, which was on this earth. Yet because that garden was ultimately forbidden to humankind, it bears about it a taint or taste of curse. Both connotations, of joy and of evil, surround the word and its use in poems like this one.

Eden as a generic term for delight is replaced by more specific garden imagery as the poem develops—in particular, that of flower and bee. Even as sexuality dominated events in the original garden, so the erotic implications of this poem's drama are emphasized. Love is the subject: the delight, the Eden in question.

But the speaker demands that it come slowly. Her first reason for reticence is that of unfamiliarity. Innocence, virginity are suggested by "Lips unused to thee" and "Bashful." Dickinson's characteristic persona in love poems is girlish, often coy. One reason for this tone, which we encounter again and again in these poems of expressed delight, is that it is biographically accurate. Whatever sexual relationships she did or did not have, the extent of their consummation in the real world of Amherst could not have been great. The bulk of activity must have taken place in the spaces of the mind. Also, I think that the tone, though its effect may be annoying, is meant to disarm, even to deceive: certainly to distract from the seriousness of the content. (This is a technique often employed by women, especially in matters of love. Women learn early not to be "threatening.")[5]

The lips, "unused," are the speaker's; the Jessamines are Eden's. Delight is to the speaker as flower is to bee. The speaker is a fainting bee, the subsequent analogy explains, who reaches late his flower. "His flower"; "her chamber." This shift in pronoun gender seems less indicative of Dickinson's homosexual tendencies[6] (she may or may not have had them, but the poem proves nothing about this issue, one way or the other), and more an instance of her use of language to identify active sexuality with the masculine, passive sexuality with the feminine. These pronouns occur in an analogy to a situation that is itself expressed in metaphor (nowhere is desire literally mentioned, nor, in fact, is the desire for a beloved *person*), so that there is little reason to take them literally. Dickinson is equally capable of turning the analogic situation around, as in the following poem.

> Spring comes on the World –
> I sight the Aprils –
> Hueless to me until thou come
> As, till the Bee
> Blossoms stand negative,
> Touched to Conditions
> By a Hum.
>   [1042]

Bee and blossom are again analogy for an erotic experience; this time, the speaker is associated with the blossom because she is waiting;

the lover is bee because he is coming. Activity and passivity are once more at issue, because they are both crucial to loving. But one may take different roles, or sides, in the process.

What seems most interesting about the bee-blossom analogy in "Come slowly—Eden!" is how, by its conclusion, it provides another reason for the speaker's desire to postpone the arrival of Eden, indicative of the powerful ambivalence that is her attraction and repulsion to delight itself. The bee, drawn by the expressly physical seductiveness of the flower—its nectar—enters her "chamber" (the sexual allusions continue) and is "lost in Balms." The bee drinks of the flower: sips the Jessamines, is lost. We have encountered those same balms in "I can wade Grief," when giants, having drunk of them, "wilt, like Men." The association of balms, so pleasurable, with liquor is habitual to Dickinson; it causes intoxication and subsequent loss of control. Here the loss is specifically located—"in Balms." Developing her poetic drama through an accumulation of images for pleasure, especially, sexual pleasure—flowers, gardens, Eden itself—Dickinson explains the reluctance of the eager but unpracticed speaker by showing the inevitable outcome of sexuality. Loss of the self. This is another poem about power. An active force with which the speaker identifies (hence the use of the masculine pronoun for the bee) is ultimately seduced and vanquished by the passive but potent force that is pleasure.

Elsewhere in the canon of Dickinson's love poetry, the amorphous propensities of pleasure, so often depicted as liquid, be it balm, liquor, or water, are explicitly shown to destroy individuality and the power of self.

Eden and the sea are identified in the concluding stanza of "Wild Nights" (249):

Rowing in Eden—
Ah, the Sea!
Might I but moor—Tonight—
In Thee!

Self is annihilated by this liquid balm, as the following lines show.

The Drop, that wrestles in the Sea—
Forgets her own locality—
As I—toward Thee—

[284]

Least Rivers – docile to some sea.
My Caspian – thee.

[212]

The drop that forgets her own locality; the river that must be subsumed, "docile," by the sea; the bee that will be lost in balms— none of these lovers are in a position to announce, "Mine – long as Ages steal!" They are possessed, not possessor. Dickinson's greatest fear emerges even in a poem like "Come slowly – Eden!," which begins with its speaker in the grip of intense pleasure. For, as the series of figures in the poem arrive at their logical conclusion, the results of pleasure become altogether too apparent.

On the one hand, delight is suspect because it ends; on the other, its lack of boundaries swallows up the one who would indulge in it. Imagery of intoxication frequently accompanies Dickinson's most dire warnings about delight, yet there is one poem in which a thoroughly inebriated speaker enjoys her lack of control and is not overcome by it: a rare portrait that develops a fantasy of achieved delight.

I taste a liquor never brewed –
From Tankards scooped in Pearl –
Not all the Vats upon the Rhine
Yield such an Alcohol!

Inebriate of Air – am I –
And Debauchee of Dew –
Reeling – thro endless summer days –
From inns of Molten Blue –

When "Landlords" turn the drunken Bee
Out of the Foxglove's door –
When Butterflies – renounce their "drams" –
I shall but drink the more!

Till Seraphs swing their snowy Hats –
And Saints – to windows run –
To see the little Tippler
Leaning against the – Sun –

[214]

The element of fantasy in this poem is pronounced; so is the presence of the ingenue persona who appears so persistently in Dickinson's love poems. The two combine to give the poem its childish air. Yet it is precisely that quality of make-believe which permits the speaker, and the poem, to maintain the happiness of which she boasts.

The poem begins with a riddle. What kind of liquor is never brewed, comes from tankards made of pearl, is far superior to any ordinary, earthly beverage? The answer: air, or dew. Even as the opening stanza clearly contrasts "real" liquor (from "Vats upon the Rhine") to another sort—not of this earth, imaginary, or symbolic, so as the poem develops its conceit of being drunk upon air, it steadily compares literal and figurative experience, experience in nature and in the mind.

Surely, air was never brewed; thus it answers the requirements of the riddle. But neither is it literally a liquor. We can interpret the metaphor: to be "Inebriate of Air" is to be exhilarated, excited, overwhelmingly delighted by summer skies. Yet as the poem elaborates this conceit, it is not its symbolism but its drama that engages the reader. When the "Debauchee of Dew" begins her drunken progress from airy inn to airy inn, her activity takes on its own reality, one that overpowers its literal counterpart. This is fantasy, and it is a delightful image. It is, in fact, an image of delight embodied.

If the extravagance of her emotion is essential to this situation, so is its lasting power. These summer days are "endless." We recall how important the idea of permanence is to Dickinson's ideal of delight.

But summer in nature's world is never endless, no matter how it may seem in mid-July. In stanza three time surfaces, only to be triumphantly repudiated by this poem's speaker. The inebriate of air has her real-life counterparts: bees and butterflies who likewise reel through the sky, with flowers as pubs; like her, drunken on the summery nectar. Yet bees and butterflies are subject to seasonal time; drinking hours are up when autumn comes.

"I shall but drink the more!" How she gets to overcome time, she doesn't say. But the final stanza shows her drinking on into eternity. "Till Seraphs swing their snowy Hats –/ And Saints to windows run –." The original riddle provides a clue, since the liquor that she drinks from opulent goblets (does "scooped in Pearl" mean that they are decorated with pearl or that the liquid that they hold is like pearl?) never was of this earth. Not "real" alcohol in the first place, its inebriation is likewise not "real"; neither are the actions to which it incites the drinker. Since her activity has always been fantasy, taking place in a mental sky, she has no difficulty perpetuating the fun. Yet her intoxication is more than fun; it is also a sign of power. In this poem, lack of control, diminutive stature, are coyly representative of their opposites, as the final audacious image, of the "little Tippler / Leaning against the – Sun –" indicates. (In another version of the line Dickinson has the little tippler "From Manzanilla come!" That makes her a world traveller; this more exciting image makes her a space traveller.)[7] She has overcome both space and time by the poem's conclusion, such is the strength, the power of her emotion. In her imagination of course, not the real world, not drinking liquor from vats upon the Rhine but one that's never brewed; yet where else does emotion happen?

This poem is another form of the celebration of delight to which I referred earlier. It perpetuates and praises the feeling, not through incantation, as in "Mine – by the Right of the White Election!" but through outright fantasy. Both poems, however, achieve their pro-longment of the emotional experience with a rhetoric that places the action of the poem in the realm of the imagination and explicitly, almost challengingly, opposes ordinary reality in the process. Here, in the space of the mind, delight can be maintained, delight can be controlled, delight can be praised.

A contrast with nature and its kind of time is an essential aspect of the poems which describe delight achieved. Although its causes can vary, love remains the primary occasion for delight. The following poem, although it is not written from *media res* and therefore lacks the drama that we have come to associate with such poems, helpfully shows, by calling attention to the artifice of its own imagery, how the experience of delight, initiated by love explicitly sexual, creates its own timeless brand of time.

> To my small Hearth His fire came –
> And all my House aglow
> Did fan and rock, with sudden light –
> 'Twas Sunrise – 'twas the Sky –
>
> Impanelled from no Summer brief –
> With limit of Decay –
> 'Twas Noon – without the News of Night –
> Nay, Nature, it was Day –
>
> [638]

Delight is not labelled as such; rather, the speaker's emotional reaction to "His fire" that has lighted her "Hearth" is expressed with a barrage of light images that are as violent as they are brilliant. Light is completely sensual, experienced without and within; it is heat, it is brilliance, it is change, an awakening that becomes total, as sunrise, which is the beginning of light after dark, turns into the skies into daylight. The explosion of light that may have begun in the speaker's "Hearth" sets off response throughout her entire "House," or self. Sexual pleasure is explicitly indicated by the imagery of this first stanza, by hearth and fire, fan and rock; yet the fact that much more than the split second of orgasmic response is meant is shown by the way in which the speaker insists, as she develops her analogies to nature and its temporal cycles, on the endlessness, the timelessness of her experience.

As the second stanza begins, the architectural metaphor that in the first stanza seems put to the service of bodily description stunningly turns to reveal how central the mind is to delight. "Impanelled": walled off, as a room is—hence protected from, immune, not subject to. Not subject to summer as it happens in nature, "With limit of Decay." (Or "license of Decay," as an alternate phrase reads.) "Noon – without the News of Night" is an eternal "Day" that is here identified as not nature's. As in so many of Dickinson's poems defining mental experience, metaphors use a vocabulary drawn from nature, because nature's events explain reality for us, yet at the same time distinguish between external and internal worlds. The enclosed space that is hearth, room, house opens wide into sunrise, sky, noon, and day, yet remains impanelled. This is because its expansion is inward, not outward. The experience of sex, of love, of delight is symbolized here by light; hence the analogies to nature's best moments of light. But this light is not timebound: it is timeless. In her final line, in which she flaunts her own creative power, the speaker calls attention to the fact that she has been in fact using analogies throughout—comparisons, words—by appropriating one of nature's words for her own quite different purposes. "Day": a brilliant, thrilling, radiant moment—that stays. Nature's day may supply the model, and the word, but the mind sees its figurative possibilities and uses it accordingly.

Poems about achieved delight, like "To my small Hearth His fire came –" and "I taste a liquor never brewed –," use a vocabulary taken from nature to talk about its opposite, a state of timelessness. When love is the occasion for delight, as it so frequently is, there are, in addition, other vocabularies that Dickinson uses persistently to describe the event. Words referring to marriage, religion, and royalty intertwine in a great many poems about love not in general but in a particular instance, *in media res.*

> Title divine – is mine!
> The Wife – without the Sign!
> Acute Degree – conferred on me –
> Empress of Calvary!
> Royal – all but the Crown!
> Betrothed – without the swoon
> God sends us Women –
> When you – hold – Garnet to Garnet –
> Gold – to Gold –
> Born – Bridalled – Shrouded –
> In a Day –
> Tri Victory
> "My Husband" – women say –
> Stroking the Melody –
> Is *this* – the way?
>
> [1072]

Dickinson's recurrent bridal imagery runs the gamut from secular to divine, from "A Wife – at Daybreak I shall be – / Sunrise – Hast thou a Flag for me?" (461) to "Given in Marriage unto Thee / Oh thou Celestial Host!" (817). Commentators tend to see the bridal images as symbolic of religious aspiration or vice versa, the heavenly images standing for earthly relationships.[8] Instead, we might think of her secular and religious terminology as interdependent ways of representing love; because for Dickinson the several forms of love, earthly and divine, can all be viewed as versions or types of the same experience.[9] Earthly love serves as a figure for heavenly love, and this is a traditional view of figure.[10] Conversely and radically, heavenly love, for Dickinson, serves as a figure for secular love. "Because God is the tenor in one set of poems and the vehicle in the other," writes Nina Baym, "we cannot interpret these poems either as strictly human or strictly divine. We are in a poetic world where the two spheres have interpenetrated, and each has lost its distinct character."[11]

What sort of love relationship is Dickinson describing here? Commentators offer variations on a similar theme. "A royal marriage," says Anderson. "The experience she is undergoing is the paradox of redemption, which involves a death to the world as well as birth to a higher spiritual life." "The life of the heavenly bride [compared] to that of the earthly one," says Cameron. In the latter, she continues, "the birth of the wife becomes the death of the woman."[12]

What is clear about the poem is that its subject is marriage; that this theme occasions contrasts between heaven and earth, death and life, royal and common. What is problematic is both how these areas of experience align (does heaven "go with" death or with life, for example?) and which words are figurative, which literal. The problem of association comes because nearly every line of the poem is grammatically parallel to every other, so that, although comparison as well as definition is essential to the meaning of the poem, it is difficult to tell which line modifies which part of a given contrast. Second, since both of the kinds of love being contrasted are identified as marriage, words like "Wife" and "Husband," "divine" and "royal," "victory" and "melody," all have both literal and figurative possibilities.

My own sense of the poem is that it celebrates the speaker's belief in the specialness of her experience of love by comparing it with that of ordinary women. Hers may be private, not public: however, it is on a higher and grander plane altogether. I think that the poem calls on its several vocabularies of spiritual and secular love in order to formulate and emphasize these distinctions, but that it is not literally about Dickinson as bride of Christ, other women as brides of men. Especially, I think that what is of primary importance about this admittedly ambiguous poem is its evocation of the emotional intensity of an experience which is surely that of love, although the particular version of it may be in question.

For the tone of exclamation, of celebration, is one aspect of the poem that is both clear and consistent, from start to finish. It is articulated with the excited rhetoric that we associate with this kind of poem, the very rhetoric that Cameron refers to with dismay as well as respect, because of its characteristic "elliptical progressions and the rapid transformation of pronouns," which can create genuine confusion for the reader.[13]

The poem begins with an exclamation of achievement, much like "Mine – by the Right of the White Election!" Achievement, however, of what? The ambiguous "Title divine" in line one is further defined in line two as that of wife, but "without the Sign." This is the poem's first comparison: to another way of being a wife, when you have a sign.

The speaker's way is further defined in a series of parallel epithets: "Acute Degree – conferred on me –"; "Empress of Calvary"; "Royal – all but the Crown"; "Betrothed – without the swoon / God sends us Women –." Each of these appellations denotes rank, and because they are in apposition, each links the marriage state with divinity and royalty. These spheres are further associated through the words that modify the epithets: *acute* degree; empress of *Calvary*. *Acute,* with its intimations of pain, fits better with *Calvary* than it does with *degree* (except as a geometrical positioning is implied); both have connections to *divine,* and to a specific aspect of divinity—the crucifixion. The speaker, then, makes claim to exalted rank for her condition, even as she admits that her claim is based on internal rather than external evidence. Each of these lines breaks at a caesura, and the second half of several of them negates external indication of rank and position: without the sign, all but the crown, without the swoon. Crown is a sign of the royal condition, and it parallels both the sign (whatever it is) of wifehood and the swoon of betrothal. What centrally defines the speaker's married state, then, is that, although of the most exalted sort (divine and royal), it is not outwardly apparent, carrying with it no symbolism or rank. Careful structural parallelism has defined an internal state by means of its external analogies and the associations between them.

With lines eight and nine, however, the clarity of the poem's parallelism is dissolved. When *do* you "hold – Garnet to Garnet –/ Gold – to Gold –"? Because this sounds like a description of wedding rings, of, consequently, a double-ring ceremony, the phrase probably modifies the swoon that God sends to women, so that swoon can be read as symbolic, or symptomatic, of the ordinary woman's response to a man, a husband, to marriage. Thus, being a wife without the sign would be being a wife without the ring—and without the swoon. No church wedding: no crown. Another sort of marriage.

The next three lines, "Born – Bridalled – Shrouded –/ In a Day –/ Tri Victory" are harder to place. Do they modify the holding of garnet to garnet, gold to gold (the literal or secular wedding of ordinary women)? Or do they modify the title divine, the wife without the sign? All of the phrases in the series do, except for the one beginning "When you – hold," which seems to be in apposition to the swoon (but that is itself located in a subordinate clause to "betrothed," which does modify "Title divine").

Both Cameron and Anderson see these lines as modifying the swoon, the secular marriage. " 'When you – hold – Garnet to Garnet – / Gold – to Gold –' (in the secular context of the earthly wedding ceremony), what you get is death ('Born – Bridalled – Shrouded – / In a Day –'). . . . For the birth of the wife becomes the death of the woman," says Cameron.[14] Anderson's interpretation is similar but more symbolic and, consequently, more idealistic. "The normal woman is 'Born – Bridalled – Shrouded – / In a Day,' the bride's whole existence being her wedding day, which brings death to the virgin and birth to the wife."[15] But why, then, "Tri Victory?" The tone of the poem is certainly one of strong affirmation of the royal, divine kind of marriage, albeit without the sign, in contrast with that of the ordinary woman, with her swoon and her wedding ring. The speaker considers herself to be "Empress of Calvary." It is she whose situation involves some version of death and resurrection. That is a victory (although it can be achieved only through the process of a birth, a marriage, and a death), because then you stay married forever, are truly powerful, "in full possession," as Anderson observes, "of the state of grace."[16] (Dickinson's bridal imagery, conjoining as it so often does the secular and the divine, frequently uses the word "grace" to characterize this state. Poem 473, for example, which begins, "I am ashamed – I hide – / What right have I – to be a Bride," continues: "Nowhere to hide my dazzled Face – / No one to teach me that new Grace – / Nor introduce – my Soul –.") Of course, a problem with the line "Born – Bridalled – Shrouded –" is that its words may be interpreted literally, or figuratively, or both. Yet if they are seen to refer to marriage, an event that involves being born, bridalled, shrouded in a day, there is no reason why they might not refer to both kinds of "marriage" that the poem is describing. If so, they will have different implications for the normal as opposed to the special marriage. And lead to a different victory.

Because, although two kinds of "marriage" are being contrasted here, we do not know at all that Dickinson means one to be, literally, that of marriage to God, the other marriage to man. She may well be using the traditional Christian imagery for the bride of Christ to characterize her sense of the profoundness of the love that she is experiencing, one which makes her seem special, set apart from other, ordinary women. We need not take "divine" literally, even as we do not take "Empress" literally. She describes here a kind of union (a marriage) that is a birth as a death (the absolute end of one state or condition); a death that is as a birth—into a day which does not end.

The poem concludes by evoking the husband himself—and the sexuality of the marriage union. Even as these lines heighten our awareness of the present tense from which the speaker writes, that she is in a marriage situation, and in it right now, they continue to underline the analogous nature of the two kinds of marriage. " 'My husband' – women say – / Stroking the Melody –." For "Melody" we can read the song that is love, which is at once the feeling and the body of the lover. For all that the speaker has distinguished herself, in her special marriage, from ordinary women, she has also allied herself, as a woman, with them and their emotional concerns: hers, too, is marriage. "Us Women," she says in line seven. Now, when it comes to the feeling itself, she underlines her affinity with women, even as she literally underlines the word "this" in the final line. "Is *this* – the way?" She, too, is in the process of stroking the melody—affirming the love, and her union with the lover. That is what the poem is about: her sense of marriage, union, love. Her sense of victory. Her feeling. With or without the sign, hers is, in her opinion, a marriage, bringing with it delight that is spiritual (divine), powerful (royal), and erotic ("Is *this* – the way?"). The poem is a celebration of that feeling.

If we grant to Dickinson's several vocabularies for depicting love an essentially figurative nature, we can understand how the imagination becomes the primary setting for love as she would have it be. As lover, she portrays herself to be royal, even divine. Images of power and of specialness conflate. But this sense of herself as both undiminished by love and as experiencing a love that will not end (the spiritual dimensions are so important because they lead to everlastingness, to being Empress of Calvary) is created by figurative language and stands in direct contrast to her knowledge of loves and marriages in the everyday world.

In a poem about this world-wise vision, "She Rose to His Requirement" (732), in which the subject takes on "the honorable Work / Of Woman, and of Wife –," the ensuing analogy between woman and sea, who are linked because of their silence and their depths, ironically establishes the fact that the woman, in her new "Day" of marriage, does indeed miss "Amplitude," "Awe," and "first Prospective."

> She rose to His Requirement – dropt
> The Playthings of Her Life

> To take the honorable Work
> Of Woman, and of Wife –
>
> If ought She missed in Her new Day,
> Of Amplitude, or Awe –
> Or first Prospective – Or the Gold
> In using, wear away,
>
> It lay unmentioned – as the Sea
> Develop Pearl, and Weed,
> But only to Himself – be known
> The Fathoms they abide –
>
>   [732]

Within—silently and privately—the woman may continue to develop self ("Pearl, and Weed"), but known only to "Himself." Dickinson uses the male pronoun for this sea, here as elsewhere, to denote qualities, such as the sense of self, that our society labels "masculine." Sandra Gilbert and Susan Gubar correctly identify these depths as "the sea of the imagination." "Irrepressible, inexorable, it silently produces pearl and weed, though such objects (like poems in a bureau drawer) are secrets known only to the strong, assertively masculine part of the woman that must be called *Him*self in a patriarchal culture."[17] On the surface, however, externally, the woman in this poem is equivalent to those women with whom the speaker of "Title divine – is mine!" contrasts herself. She is the one who possesses the sign; however, the gold of that wedding ring is worn away by the "honorable" work of woman, and wife.

The irony of the poem's perspective is thoroughgoing. Even as, through its manipulation of analogical implications, it exposes the traditional goal, and life, of most women as destructive, reductive, so it undercuts, as well, the traditional meanings allotted to the transition that must occur between childhood and adulthood. In the first stanza, the childlife of the young woman is placed in clear contrast to her newly acquired adult status, "Playthings" exchanged for real "Work." Yet via the "slant" of the subjunctive, the second stanza assigns qualities more usually associated with maturity to childhood: "Amplitude," "Awe," "Prospective." Gilbert and Gubar identify these qualities as "products of the sea of the imagination." "From Dickinson's point of view," they continue, "Amplitude and Awe are the only absolute necessities. 'I always ran home to Awe, when a child, if anything befell me,' she told Higginson once."[18] As in poems diverse as "I taste a liquor never brewed" and "Delight is as the Flight –," childhood and childishness are associated with both power and vision. Induction into adult womanhood is seen as a birth that becomes a death: female sexuality incurs death of self, death of soul, what Gilbert and Gubar term "the symbolic castration implicit in female powerlessness."[19]

The adult poet's assumption of a child persona, or a childish point of view, is one way by which she yokes delight to the only setting where it can be nurtured and sustained, the imagination. " 'If it would last'/I asked the East,/When that Bent Stripe/Struck up my child-ish/Firmament –." "Childish" is the key word. It stands for innocence, optimism, naiveté, vulnerability, and an inability or disinclination to make firm distinctions between "fantasy" and "reality."

The perspective of childhood is central to the following paired poems, as are the other vocabularies that we have come to associate with delight in all its difficulties: marriage, religion, and nature in its cycles, especially that of day and night. The dimensional vocabulary so frequently used by Dickinson to chart mental space provides a superstructure for possession and loss equivalent to that of rainbows and empty skies. These are poems of *media res*, their composite narrative dramatizing the complete process that the pursuit of delight occasions.

A Wife – at Daybreak I shall be –
Sunrise – Hast thou a Flag for me?
At Midnight, I am but a Maid,
How short it takes to make a Bride –
Then – Midnight, I have passed from thee
Unto the East, and Victory –

Midnight – Good Night! I hear them call,
The Angels bustle in the Hall –
Softly my Future climbs the Stair,
I fumble at my Childhood's prayer
So soon to be a Child no more –
Eternity, I'm coming – Sir,
Savior – I've seen the face – before!

[461]

Good Morning – Midnight –
I'm coming Home –
Day – got tired of Me –
How could I – Of Him?

Sunshine was a sweet place –
I liked to stay –

But Morn – didn't want me – now –
So – Goodnight – Day!

I can look – can't I –
When the East is Red?
The Hills – have a way – then –
That puts the Heart – abroad –

You – are not so fair – Midnight –
I chose – Day –
But – please take a little Girl –
He turned away!

[425]

Although it is understandable why the conflation of temporal, spatial, secular, and religious imagery in these poems might lead to interpreting them as about earth and heaven, living and dying, when the poems are viewed together, the consistency of their themes and patterns makes a reading like John Todd's of "Good Morning – Midnight –" unconvincing: "Day seems to stand for life in the poem and midnight, death."[20] Dickinson's symbolism, though never a matter of one-to-one correlations, and never rigidly codified, is predictably and generally patterned, as Rebecca Patterson and others have shown.[21] In these two poems written in the same year, it is unlikely that daybreak will stand for death, midnight for life in poem 461, and then for life in poem 425 ("Day – got tired of Me –"), with midnight meaning death. Rather, I think that both poems are about love, and together they represent the movement from before to during to after, or from not having to having to not having again. Temporal and spatial designation, like daybreak and midnight, east and west, function as symbolic compass points to mark the process.

Nevertheless, because these poems are about love, they are about death, although not in the literal sense that Todd employs. Love *is* death in Dickinson's eyes: death to the virgin and to the child; death to the self. Even as "Title divine – is mine" is about love as death, even as "She rose to his Requirement –" is about love as death, so "A Wife – at Daybreak I shall be –" is about the relation between love and death.

The poem explicitly and immediately provides a setting in time and space for emotional experience. Marriage and daybreak are equated in line one, virginity and midnight in line three. Both dimensions define the poem's movement, for daybreak is "the East" and midnight, by implication, the west. The speaker takes a journey that is a climb, short but steep: "How short it takes to make a Bride – / Then –

Midnight, I have passed from thee / Unto the East, and Victory –";
"Softly my Future climbs the Stair." (Day is a familiar location in
Dickinson's poems for love. When his fire came to her small hearth,
"it was Day" (638). Day is when the more ordinary wife in "Title
divine – is mine!" is born, bridalled, and shrouded. Likewise, marriage equals "Her new Day" in "She rose to his Requirement –.")

The first stanza is structured by martial as well as marital imagery. The achievement of marriage is seen as a victory, with a flag to
prove it. The speaker is confident of both her success and her goal.
But the second stanza changes tack, and tone, substituting for the
warrior's stance a child's voice and perspective. Having bid farewell to
"Midnight," the speaker pauses before she arrives at daybreak. While
her "Future" climbs the stair, while "Angels" bustle in the hall, she
stays in her childhood room: fumbling, she says, at her "Childhood's
prayer." With angels in the hall and eternity as the future to be encountered, we are tempted to identify that childish prayer with the
familiar "Now I lay me down to sleep" of our own childhood. Is she,
then, about to die before she wakes? Is there, in other words, some
apprehension towards the "victory" that the speaker in stanza one
appropriated so confidently as her own? A reluctance to take the flag
which may well stand for a death not literal but nonetheless true?

Although ambivalence is manifest, her pause is a brief one. By
the end of the stanza she has turned to face her future. In stanza one
she does this, too, speaking confidently to sunrise. Here the object of
her address is "Eternity," "Sir," "Savior." Is he, then, God, appearing
in Heaven after she has died? This seems too simplistic an explanation. As I have pointed out, Dickinson's erotic vocabulary is filled with
exaltations of a beloved who is sometimes obviously divine and sometimes obviously not and most of the time a curious blend of both.
Again it seems best and most accurate to assert that Dickinson associated love with the divine, and granted to the beloved (whoever)
god-like power. (In the two other variants of this poem, the appella-
tion "Savior" is replaced by "Master." This is Dickinson's name for the
unknown but surely human recipient of her most passionate letters.
Yet Dickinson's "Master" had as much power, to her, as any god.)

In this instance the arrival of sunrise, which becomes, in the
process of the poem, eternal, is equivalent to entering Heaven, a
heaven altogether familiar: "I've seen the face before!" Although this
is the same husband whom the speaker was about to join in stanza

one, the conditions of the marriage have subtly altered. Eternity has replaced flux—for if sunrise succeeds midnight, then midnight ought at some usual point to succeed sunrise. But not in the newly defined terms of this poem. For "Victory" is not enough, which the pause at childhood's final threshhold has perhaps indicated to the speaker. We do not hear the words of her prayer; we have only the poem, where "Eternity, I'm coming – Sir" replaces "Unto the East – and Victory –" in parallel positions, to show us that a change has occurred.

If the angels in the hall are symptomatic of death, that is not only because love and death are irrevocably associated for Dickinson, but because love must somehow be translated into timelessness for it to be tolerable. If love can triumph over time, the self lost through the death that is love can be regained. If time can be turned into eternity, with the self in charge of that apotheosis, "Day" can become "endless summer days"; "Noon – without the News of Night."

In the second poem, however, the imagination's power to posit eternity has abruptly failed: delight is finished. The speaker must return to her life without it. Again, day and night and their associated compass points are used to situate this emotional event in space and time. In this poem day and night are themselves personified, so that place, time, and agent unite in intense polarity. Love gained; love lost: ambivalence is not relevant now.

The poem begins with a stated paradox that is in miniature an embodiment of the complete configuration of the speaker's situation: "Good Morning – Midnight –." If day has become night, and we soon learn that it has, because day is he, who "got tired" of her, then time has been returned to the scenario—and with it, the inevitability of loss. To try to turn night into day, as she does when she says, "Good morning" to it, is, in this instance, pathetic, not powerful, because when this poem begins, the speaker has already lost the battle to replace literal truth with the truth of the imagination. Particularly poignant is the fact that the midnight she was so eager to leave in "A Wife – at Daybreak I shall be –," that place where she was "but a Maid," must now be identified as "Home." Home is thus no comfort but the place of pain, and loss, because day got tired of her: "How could I – Of Him?"

The second stanza reiterates, surely for emphasis, the statement of the first, ending with an inverted version of the opening paradox. Sunshine was sweet, she "liked to stay," but wasn't wanted, "now."

"So – Goodnight – Day!" Even as the first stanza cannot turn night into day with rhetoric, so the apostrophe in the second stanza is a recognition that, hereafter, day must be night.

The compass points that embody the speaker's condition provide an appropriate although simple symbolism. Day, equated with the beloved, has synonyms, like "Sunshine" and "Morn"; in stanza three, it is fair with the color of dawn, red. Red is as well the color of the heart, and, watching the sunrise ("I can look – can't I –?"), the speaker is still very much in love, her heart reaching towards him. Red is also the color of blood, of pain. In this poem, each of red's symbolic equivalents engenders the other; for surely the heart abroad, drawn to the east, is a bleeding heart.

The speaker finishes by telling patient Midnight the truth, that it is second-best: "You – are not so fair." Yet where else can she turn but back, since "He turned away." "Please take a little girl," she concludes, using, as she has throughout, the child persona so persistent in these poems. For the loss of love is a return to childhood, to the dark middle of the night that has all along been associated with a virginal state. Dickinson may be loath, at times, to surrender girlhood; and she may cling to its qualities, for protection and even power, as she attempts to deal with that most difficult of conditions, love and delight. But she also recognizes its limitations, especially when she has lost control of the situation and is being returned, not returning of her own accord.

The paired poems form a chart of anticipation and loss. In both the speaker is situated in midnight, her sights set on day. The temporal cycle that occurs within the duration of the poems posits but does not describe the experience of day. It diagrams location; conditions; attitude. Yet day is at all times the focus of the speaker's aspirations and disillusionment. Although not described here, we know it, from both the symbolism of these poems and from other of Dickinson's poems that do try to bring it into the realm of words, to be the incarnation of love and delight. These two poems are useful in documenting for us the span of the "flight" itself; from the present tense of expectation, of desire, situated in time, to the present tense of loss and pain, situated once again in time.

The flight, however, does occur, as does "the instant / We achieve the Joy –." Some of Dickinson's poems, written as it happens, from its setting, day, from *media res,* keep it aloft through sheer power of the imagination, manifested with a rhetoric of celebration and fantasy. When the flight does not end.

3

That it does end is shown by other poems, written from the perspective of afterwards, when "Our portion in the fashion –" is "Done –." Dickinson may expend huge amounts of energy protecting herself from the possibilities of "empty skies." Sometimes she insulates herself from the pain of loss by permitting herself desire but never its fulfillment. Sometimes, in those poems which do an about-face and present delight, magically achieved, she can, through the exercise of imaginative will and poetic skill, deny the existence of any afterwards by creating a timeless space of happiness without end, where rainbows *are* the common way. Yet there are also poems in her canon that attest to the existence of an afterwards and to her experience of it.

The voice that speaks these poems no longer exclaims, as it did *in media res*. It pronounces, asserting that what it says are general truths. Yet these poems differ in tone and vocabulary from those I have called the poems of definition, like "Expectation – is Contentment –" or "Satisfaction – is the Agent / Of Satiety –," which speak from an unlocated before and which provide extensive argument for why one should not, in the first place, venture onto delight's terrain. Poems from afterwards have an experiential rather than a theoretical locus: they have been there. Their imagery, for example, is more concrete, more dramatically realized: "To put this World down, like a Bundle – / And walk steady, away, / Requires Energy –" (527); "Although I put away his life – / An Ornament too grand / For Forehead low as mine, to wear" (366). The world that one can, through sheer power of will, diminish to the size of a bundle, the life that is brilliant and rich, a grand ornament, are known entities and depicted as such.

To discuss delight from the vantage point of afterwards, Dickinson once again finds ratio to be her fundamental principle of measurement. Proportion is essential for defining the relationship between two times, now and then; between two situations, loss and delight.

Rehearsal to Ourselves
Of a Withdrawn Delight –

Affords a Bliss like Murder –
Omnipotent – Acute –

We will not drop the Dirk –
Because We love the Wound
The Dirk Commemorate – Itself
Remind Us that we died.

[379]

If delight means life (in this poem it does), its loss must be death. Consequently, the pleasure afforded by pretending to be still alive is at the same time a reenactment of the inevitable death. Self-imposed this time, it is still a murder.

One reaction to the loss of delight is to perpetuate, by means of the imagination, its presence. Dickinson begins by calling this action "Rehearsal." As well as pointing to the element of pretense in this situation, the word *rehearsal* also seems to skew our perspective on time, since traditionally rehearsals occur before and not after an event. And yet there is a logic to this use of the term, since rehearsals are by definition not, ever, the actual event, even as this enactment can never be exactly the withdrawn delight. Memory as rehearsal is anticipatory, not static, and it leads to a resolution: each time the loss again, the pain, the death.

For the bliss created by this rehearsal is intrinsically intertwined with loss. It is "like Murder": death-dealing, because it contains within itself the certain knowledge of its inevitable end. (Desiring without possessing delight, one need never experience loss; in the midst of delight, one can perpetuate the seeming timelessness of the present; but after delight has ended, one's experience of it is forever involved with the experience of loss.) The bliss is both "omnipotent" (powerful) and "acute" (intense, sharp).

In the second stanza the rehearsal becomes, through metonymy, a knife. The original delight is portrayed as a wound (it caused, after all, the speaker's emotional, psychic death). The conceit that the second stanza develops explains why one would keep on recreating the bliss, when, knife-like, it hurts, too. Pretending causes one to experience both the pleasure and the pain; but it keeps one experiencing. "The Wound / The Dirk Commemorate" may remind us that we died, but the act of commemoration is itself a constant resurrection. Without it, without the rehearsal, the pretending, one stays dead: i.e., numb, devoid of feeling. The act of the imagination is here considered as less real, shadow of a form, than the original experience—it is pretending or rehearsal only—but *only* is enough to bring the dead to life. Even if, in fidelity to the drama which it rehearses, the death, too, must be continually reenacted.

From the perspective of afterward, as from *media res*, one tactic available to the mind is to try to control the process of time. Memory, although it may be viewed as shadow in ratio to a previous form, yet keeps the past alive: in this way it stops time. "No Passenger was known to flee –/ That lodged a night in memory –," writes Dickinson in a late, concise assessment of the matter: "That wily – subterranean Inn / Contrives that none go out again –" (1406). But memory's power is double-edged: as the previous poem indicates, it can imprison the thinker as well as the event. Dickinson's well-known analysis of remorse, as "Memory – awake –/ Her Parties all astir –" (744) concludes by equating the perpetual incarnation of an event that must be observed as well as relived ("Past – set down before the Soul / And lighted with a Match –") with a disease that has no cure, a living hell:

> Remorse is cureless – the Disease
> Not even God – can heal –
> For 'tis His institution – and
> The Adequate of Hell –

The understanding that virtuous behavior (feeling remorse), God's institution, brings about an equivalence of hell only underlines once again how complex is Dickinson's assessment of Christian stringencies. Yet she knows, because she does have Puritan sources, and also because she is a woman, a way to achieve power over memory, to use it for her own ends. This is the strategy of renunciation, the "piercing Virtue" (745), the "long 'Nay'–" (349). Renunciation brings memory to heel, using it to alter the future. Renunciation may be a negative as well as a piercing virtue, but it is not passive. It "Requires Energy – possibly Agony –" (527). It is not simply a rephrasing of the position articulated in the "poems of definition," i.e., don't do it. Dickinson's poems of renunciation, based as they are upon having, in fact, done it, use the experience of delight and subsequent loss to control the future.

Renunciation's clear source in Christian theology is acknowledged by Dickinson herself in poems like 527, when she identifies it as "the Scarlet way / Trodden with straight renunciation / By the Son of

God –." That poem goes on to describe other travellers on the path, Christ's "faint Confederates," and to label the act as "Sacrament." Yet Dickinson, here as always, is no mere follower of proscribed dictates; she puts renunciation to her own purposes. Karl Keller argues for "a tense ambiguity in our understanding of her Puritan origins. She stamps her foot at what she stands on. She yells at the voice she yells with. Like the Brahma, it is with Puritan wings themselves that she has the power to flee the Puritan past." "One finds in her," Keller observes, "the stereotypic Puritan psychology," including "the prideful self-satisfaction of renunciation." Yet this is not "mere renunciation," he argues, "but esthetic use of what she morally and intellectually rejects. Renunciation is passive, but her uses of Edwards' pit are creative, aggressive. Her discovery was that she could use one set of things (the dark Puritanism she learned and left) as spur for another set (freedom, excitement, a sensed life, fulfillment)." Most importantly, Keller observes that "Puritanism was for her a norm of language from which her individual speech diverged into literature."[22] That is, as I have observed before, her Puritan heritage persistently provided her with a vocabulary, with metaphors, for experience that she and her world understood.

In addition, as Sandra Gilbert and Susan Gubar have pointed out, an "aesthetics of renunciation" in nineteenth-century poetry by women articulated "that graceful or passionate self-abnegation which, for a nineteenth-century woman, was necessity's highest virtue."[23] Yet again, Dickinson rings essential changes; her psychological and literary use of this aspect of her female birthright was not the same as that destruction of the assertive, creative self which poets like Christina Rossetti, and novelists like George Eliot, proscribe for their heroines.[24] For Dickinson's endorsement of the strategy of renunciation, though neither consistent nor unambivalent, did give her a control over the shape of her life, both present and future, which Rossetti and Eliot explicitly deny to Laura and to Dorothea at the conclusion of their narratives.

"Negation without loss," is what Sharon Cameron calls this gesture, identifying it with sacrifice, one of the fundamental tenets of Christianity: "the loss of the desired object and its subsequent reinstatement, the relinquishing of a part for the promise of a regained whole, Abraham's hope that God might be bargained with."[25] The phrase, "without loss," is crucial, for it points to what distinguishes renunciation from memory as an agent that can control time. "Rehearsal to Ourselves/Of a Withdrawn Delight," for example, shows that while memory alone can reenact the bliss, it cannot forget the loss. The bargain that renunciation transacts, however, in each of several ways, demands the eradication of loss.

First, if one gives up the desired object, the delight, oneself, then one cannot be rejected. Further, the poem which follows shows how this act may itself be a prelude to repossession, but on different terms.

Although I put away his life—
An Ornament too grand
For Forehead low as mine, to wear,
This might have been the Hand

That sowed the flower, he preferred—
Or smoothed a homely pain,
Or pushed the pebble from his path—
Or played his chosen tune—

On Lute the least—the latest—
But just his Ear could know
That whatsoe'er delighted it,
I never would let go—

The foot to bear his errand—
A little Boot I know—
Would leap abroad like Antelope—
With just the grant to do—

His weariest Commandment—
A sweeter to obey,
Than "Hide and Seek"—
Or skip to Flutes—
Or All Day, chase the Bee—

Your Servant, Sir, will weary—
The Surgeon, will not come—
The World, will have its own—to do—
The Dust, will vex your Fame—

The Cold will force your tightest door
Some February Day,
But say my apron brings the sticks
To make your Cottage gay—

That I may take that promise
To Paradise, with me—
To teach the Angels, avarice,
You, Sir, taught first—to me.

[366]

Dickinson's ostensible and initial reason for renouncing possession of delight ("his life") is that she is not worthy of her lover. Yet we cannot help but be suspicious of this explanation, because the role that she immediately projects for herself, the one she would fill if she had not "put it away," is one of servant to master, child to adult. Its primary requirement is precisely a "Forehead low." But unworthiness turns out not to be the only reason for renunciation given in the poem. The other comes later, in the final stanza, after an extended fantasy that, as it proceeds, succeeds in altering the tenets with which it began. Only then does the speaker offer a second reason, which is that she may keep possession of her "avarice" (or desire for him): perpetuating it by teaching it to the very angels in heaven (thus sabotaging a conventional heaven even as she has, in the course of the poem, managed to sabotage the earthly fate that might well have been hers if she had not "put away his life").

For it is the rhetorical structure, itself, of the poem that creates the "negation without loss" of renunciation. By means of her linguistic tactics, the speaker gets to keep the very thing she says she has given up, but on her own terms. Terms which, however, require a mental rather than a societal setting for their fulfillment.

Shifting from the indicative to the subjunctive mood as the first stanza concludes, the speaker makes a lengthy list of the activities that she would have undertaken had she *not* put away his life. These include pushing pebbles from his path, bearing his errands, obeying his "weariest" commands. The long list of services takes four stanzas. Everything about the list helps to create a portrait of a diminished person in a subservient role. Synecdoche reduces the "person" to but an assortment of parts: a hand, a foot. This little person is both slave and child: obeying his commandments would be "sweeter" than playing hide and seek, skipping to flutes, chasing bees. True, this servant-lover is exceptionally *good* at her tasks—much better, she observes in stanza six, than anyone or anything else, including servants, doctors, world, and time itself. Nevertheless, her very excellence requires a selflessness seemingly at odds with the personality whose strong will would renounce the one she loves. (However, they may be viewed as two sides of the same coin, or woman: "Energy—possibly Agony—" put to different purposes.) Surely, what Dickinson is portraying here, emphasizing by exaggeration, is the traditional female role, by which she is both attracted and repelled. (She likes to feel the love; she does not like to feel the loss of self.) This poem shows her first rejecting it; then experiencing it imaginatively, in the subjunctive mood.

In stanza six there comes a turn in the poem. Suddenly the speaker switches from subjunctive to indicative mood, from narrative to direct address, speaking, although she has ostensibly renounced her lover, to him as though he were right there with her: "Sir." But of course here in the place of the imagination she has been experiencing having, not losing, his life; so that here he may be privy to her present tense. Now she makes another list for him, demonstrating how literal time and literal world will bring him down to death, "Some February Day." (The symbolic progression from servant wearying to surgeon not coming to world having its way to dust vexing his fame makes cold forcing his tightest door emblematic of death.) Yet *she* is capable of lighting a fire in his deathly cottage, of giving him new life in heaven, the speaker maintains. (If he will give her permission to do so. Which seems, at this point in the narrative, more an order than a request.) She will take that promise with her, she says, to Paradise: "To teach the Angels, avarice, / You, Sir, taught first – to me." Neatly reversing their roles, she shows that she has given him up in one world to keep him in another, where it will be greed, not humility (self, not selfless-ness) that will get her what she has wanted all along: him. But now hers will be a position of power, not lack of it. And she will have him forever.

For if she were to "teach the Angels, avarice," she would be redefining another traditional institution, heaven, so that, forever after, she might experience the love situation on her own terms. This "Paradise," like the poem's earlier construction of an experience which was literally not, is introduced by the subjunctive: "That I may take." It functions in the poem as the imagined future towards which this narrative has developed: a timeless state in which the self might possess delight without loss, power with love.

As "Although I put away his life" surely indicates, central to renunciation's power is its ability to manipulate and to control time. In the following poem, renunciation allows one to sacrifice the future to the past, thereby creating a present in which, once again, loss has not and will not occur.

I had the Glory – that will do –
An Honor, Thought can turn her to

When lesser Fames invite –
With one long "Nay" –
Bliss' early shape
Deforming – Dwindling – Gulfing up –
Time's possibility.

[349]

Although this poem takes a generalized, proclamatory stance towards the mind's control of the relationship between past and future,
bliss and loss, its opening line establishes the personal, experiential
basis for its subsequent remarks. "Had" and "Glory" share emphasis
in the first half of the line, so that not delight in the abstract but
delight once possessed is at issue here. On the other side of the caesura, "that" and "do" share the emphasis. "That" refers not to "Glory"
alone as subject of the poem but to the act of having it. "Do" is in the
future tense, equally active, establishing a connection between past
and future that bridges but ignores the present.

Two parallel phrases in apposition to this first one define how the
mind, "Thought," negotiates between past and future to create a
present that stymies both. In the first, having had the glory is shown
to be "An Honor" to which thought can turn when "lesser Fames
invite." The speaker can reject those lesser fames, because none are
up to what she once had. They are easily refused, in fact, because
when they are encountered, the mind's response is to turn to, remember, thus reexperience, the glory it had.

Having the glory is further defined as "Bliss' early shape." Lesser
can be conceived of spatially as well as morally, so that the largeness of
the original experience can be used by the mind to affect any future
event, "Time's possibility." The mind can deform, dwindle, gulf it up.
Thus the second half of the poem, its second appositional phrase, is
not truly parallel to the first, because it reveals how "lesser Fames" can
be rendered so by the mind's activities upon them. Thought, as it acts
out renunciation, can alter the very nature of subsequent events, can
minimize them so that they will never be as large, as significant as the
original "Glory." Saying no to time's possibility permits the mind to
design a future, one that is immune to the world's incursions upon it.
For although the long "Nay" has cut out all new chances for bliss, it
has also blocked all new chances for loss. In this way it perpetuates the
original glory, albeit once removed, into the present and, thus, the
future.

Renunciation is, essentially, a negotiation for the future. Loss in the present can buy a future without it.

Renunciation – is a piercing Virtue –
The letting go
A Presence – for an Expectation –
Not now –
The putting out of Eyes –
Just Sunrise –
Lest Day –
Day's Great Progenitor –
Outvie
Renunciation – is the Choosing
Against itself –
Itself to justify
Unto itself –
When larger function –
Make that appear –
Smaller – that Covered Vision – Here –

[745]

Dickinson's most famous statement on renunciation is composed in terms of spatial and temporal ratio: between "Presence" and "Expectation," between "Sunrise" and a heavenly light, between "larger function" and "Smaller," between "itself" and "itself." This poem's manipulation of distances that are both extreme and intimate dramatizes renunciation's purpose and its difficulty.

Purpose and difficulty are neatly compressed into the oxymoronic aphorism with which the poem begins, and they are explicated by the parallel analogues that comprise the body of the poem. Renunciation is a virtue; renunciation is piercing. The image of sharp penetration, of wound and subsequent pain, makes immediate connection with renunciation's Christian sources, with the ur-renunciation, Christ's own sacrifice. That suffering is a virtue, that virtue should be achieved through suffering are not unfamiliar axioms.

"The pain of the conflict is woven into the first three lines and enacted in the direct discourse of 'Not now –,'" observes Cameron.[26] The force of this pain is continued by the analogy which follows, as it turns the idea of piercing into an image of self-inflicted blinding, "The putting out of Eyes." Dickinson's point (no pun intended) is that the delights of the physical world of the present, its sunrise and day, must be "overlooked"—not looked at—in order that one might see, at a subsequent date, another kind of light: that of "Day's Great Progenitor," who is surely God; thus a light heavenly or spiritual. That the two lights are competitive is essential. Otherwise there is no sacrifice, hence no virtue involved. That the two lights are *different* is also essential. Renunciation is not about giving up chicken on Sunday so that you might have it on Wednesday. You give up chicken altogether, but you get—maybe ice cream. Here Dickinson describes the situation in terms of earth and heaven, because heaven is the appropriate emblem of the future as an altered state in the Christian context that the poem establishes. Yet, since Dickinson's prevailing attitude toward heaven is always less than orthodox, here, too, her use of Christian terminology may serve metaphoric purpose. ("Vinnie says you are most illustrious and dwell in Paradise," she writes in a letter to Mrs. Holland. "I have never believed the latter to be a superhuman site."[27]) In this poem, we interpret "expectation," the light created by "Day's Great Progenitor," and the place, different from "Here," where "larger function" is revealed, as "Heaven." The label fits with the poem's symbolic vocabulary. But noting its symbolic function, we might think of "Heaven" as a concept, neither a literal city with angels at the gates nor a literal life-after-death.

In line eleven the poem offers another definition of renunciation: "the Choosing / Against itself." While the first nine lines explain renunciation by expanding distances and underlying differences (between expectation and presence, between heaven and earth), these lines contract distance to reveal intimate association. The choosing is against itself, so that presence and expectation, heaven and earth are shown to be aspects of itself—or oneself, the one who does the choosing. Renunciation may be viewed as an internal journey from one "place" in the mind to another, from one tense in the mind to another, from one interpretation of experience to another. Interpretation is a form of vision. From the perspective of a future of "larger function," "Here" will be revealed as smaller, a situation of "Covered Vision." (The other words that Dickinson considered here for "Covered"—"flooded" and "sated"—expand the implications of her difficulty with the everyday world. Like a "Covered Vision," a "flooded – Vision" "knows – it cannot see –"; "sated," it is deadly near to being "Contented as Despair –.") But one needs uncovered sight to see that one's vision has been covered, and self-sacrifice, self-inflicted pain is required. One must cover, blind, the covered vision to see differently. The action is worth nothing if the choice is easy, or simple. The fact that itself must choose against its very self (one aspect of self against another) is what makes justification (another term from Puritan theology[28]) possible.

With the full power of Puritan expression behind her, but turned to her own purposes, Dickinson is talking about giving up certain experiences as they happen in the literal world, the external world, the world of "Day" in all its genuine albeit transitory appeal, that they might happen, but differently, in the world of the mind. For example, the experience of delight, which cannot be sustained in the outside world, but which can be perpetuated within. This is one aspect of what Keller means when he speaks of Dickinson using Puritanism as a spur for "freedom, excitement, a sensed life, fulfillment." Keller describes her "emerging through language to her little epiphanies. She could have her heaven *now*. But these are heavens of her own poetic making."[29]

Renunciation leads Dickinson to a future of her own making. Delight may well be "as the flight," but there is one way to put oneself at the other end of the rainbow, to be there at those "latitudes far on." Dickinson's poems of renunciation show her organizing her desire for delight in relation to her fear of lack of boundaries; her need for permanence in relation to her fear of loss; her commitment to suffering as a means to personal goals. Renunciation, like poem 745, begins with an acute awareness of the distance between having and not having, desire and loss, past and present, past and future, but ends by showing how the mind's energy, and will, and power can change the ratios, alter the proportions, so that one gets what one wants.

The final poem that follows, another definition of delight, is also constructed in terms of spatial relationships, even as was the poem with which this chapter began, "Delight is as the flight." It measures, however, the ratio between center and circumference (land to the sea that circles it, now to the future that circles it). This different vision offers a circular rather than a linear vision of time and space: not the arrow flight of the rainbow, into latitudes far on, but something else. Eternity—"duration or continuance without beginning or end," to quote Dickinson's dictionary[30]—and·the exultation, intoxication, the delight, with which it is associated, is located at the far edge of where one is. Within its analogy of journey from land to sea, this poem does not examine methodology—the nature or technique of the journey,

as have many of the poems in this chapter. But it does show delight to
be possessable, eternity to be available, and the two to be aspects of
one another.

Exultation is the going
Of an inland soul to sea,
Past the houses – past the headlands –
Into deep Eternity –

Bred as we, among the mountains,
Can the sailor understand
The divine intoxication
Of the first league out from land?
[76]

V *"Costumeless Consciousness"*

ETERNITY IS THE GOAL of the journey. This fact is never at issue for Dickinson. She is sure that experience, emotional adventures like delight and pain, have a purpose that goes beyond sensation, even knowledge. The events that comprise experience make the path to eternity. The metaphor of journey is omnipresent: "Past the houses – past the headlands – / Into deep Eternity –" (76); "The Road to Paradise is plain" (1491).

> Our journey had advanced –
> Our feet were almost come
> To that odd Fork in Being's Road –
> Eternity – by Term –
>
> [615]

A movement is always implicit. What is problematic for Dickinson throughout her life is not the travel but its direction, the location of eternity. Where? "Is Heaven a Place – a Sky – a Tree? / . . . Where – Omnipresence – fly?" (489).

To encounter this ultimate question, Dickinson begins, as always, with the tenets of her Christian heritage: with the promise of heaven. In her writing "Eternity," "Immortality," "Heaven," "Paradise" are not words between which she makes fine distinctions. The familiar vocabulary will do: keys on which to play the tunes of her choice.[1] What tunes, however? These can vary, for the distinctions to be drawn here need to identify this most evasive truth. "Are you certain there is another life," she writes to Charles Clark in 1883: "When

133

overwhelmed to know, I fear that few are sure."[2] A happy Christian heaven, the security of life after death, can be neither forgotten nor accepted. Her writing, as many have observed, presents the full gamut of answers to that worried question, from qualified affirmation ("This World is not Conclusion. / A Species stands beyond –" [501]) to qualified denial ("Paradise is of the option"[3]). More important, as I have suggested, is the concern of the poems not with the matter of "if" but with the twin puzzles of "where" and "when," since location is both spatial and temporal. It is true that Dickinson investigates the fact of dying so assiduously in order that she may catch a glimpse, through sheer imaginative will, of what lies beyond. It is true that she examines and reexamines her catechism, in the hope that the old stories, the old beliefs, will yield new insight. But it is equally true that there exists a body of poems and statements attesting to a consciousness of eternity now. An eternity experienced in life and situated in the space of the mind.

These are the poems I will investigate, with the understanding that they do not represent the totality of her explorations of the issue of eternity. What they do represent most fully, however, is an essential aspect of the depiction and revelation of the mind that her poems as a body offer. For its location as eternity turns out to be one of the mind's most significant features.

Exploration of the "Undiscovered Continent" is a life's enterprise. Not less than eternity defines the ultimate perimeters of the mental landscape: paradoxically, it may seem, both its center and its edges. To put it another way, engagement with intensest psychic experience brings one, sometimes, to the limits of experience, to the extremes of the mind: which become limitless. Eternity is situated at precisely those latitudes where the mind opens out upon itself, to become vast and endless, as immense as the universe. Where space and time desist. Thus the very endeavor to locate, to fix and situate with language the place of eternity, brings one to illocality, or abstraction incarnate.

Robert Weisbuch calls Dickinson's notion of eternity in life "temporal eternity" or "experiential eternity": "Dickinson's idea of experiential eternity leaps over the grave, negates Judgment, and insists that the mind's circumference *is* the ultimate circumference." Sharon Cameron calls it "immortality" which is "purified of all but created soul" and describes Dickinson's "belief that immortality not only will

replace an inadequate temporal scheme in the future that is promised
by a traditional Christianity . . . but also that it does replace temporality
in the present, as the body is transcended in the phenomena of loss
and immortality alike." Albert Gelpi remarks succinctly: "As a psychological state, 'Heaven' is the furthest dimension of selfhood."[4] All
three writers point to the mental, non-corporeal aspect of eternity,
what I am calling abstract. Eternity as it happens in the mind is the
embodiment of thought at its most purely conceptual. I use the word
"embodiment" because the experience does happen, is real, and yet of
course the idea of corporeality is the opposite of absolute abstraction.
Eternity, in fact, is the place where what I have called the "dimensional" and "conceptual" aspects of the mind, and of the language
Dickinson creates to talk about mental experience, come into ultimate
conjunction, often collision.

Cameron calls Dickinson's attempts to talk about eternity "language . . . flung out into the reaches of the unknown in the apparent
hope that it might civilize what it finds there." Yes, and the job she
does is extraordinary if not perfect, because finally, eternity while it is
being experienced is without language: "For immortality as Dickinson
dreams it into existence is not simply specified as permanence; it is
also presence liberated from the mortal encumbrances of both flesh
and language," says Cameron.[5] Nevertheless, it needs to be talked
about. Language is the only way to find out what, especially where, it
is; language is the only way, before or after the experience, to reveal
to others its significance.

Language's best procedure for ascertaining location is speculation, or supposition, or hypothesis. Dickinson seeks other sources: the
received truths of public doctrine (Christianity), the facts of empirical
knowledge (science). What she finds when she follows their procedures is inaccurate and inappropriate. She counters the public with
the personal, the fact with the possibility, the certain with the uncertain. Speculation is realized in language with analogy. Analogies allow
one to use concrete forms to incarnate the abstract while understanding at the same time their figurative nature.

Nevertheless, the concrete and abstract properties of language
come into collisions often violent when Dickinson ceases to hypothesize about possible or potential location and tries to describe
eternity experienced. She frequently creates metaphors that cannot
be imaged, although they point to, create a sense of the utterly ab-

stract. Concrete and abstract come close to destroying one another when they get this close; these analogies for eternity are the extremes of Dickinson's linguistic program for describing mental space. After them would come silence: the silence of death or of total vision.

Because eternity is that situation of mind most abstract and most pure, poems about eternity turn out to be poems that define the mind's ultimate potential and essential nature. When consciousness expands fully, braving death in all of its versions, both the literal and the figurative, it comes to its widest and most focused state, which is eternity.

1

Poems that search for eternity incarnate a conceptual tension between here (known) and there (unknown). They follow the path of speculation, and they use analogy, with its words that are concrete and dimensional, precisely because they need to see, to know, and yet their subject is so "fickle," as Dickinson says in poem 1195.

"Exultation is the going / Of an inland soul to sea" (76), the poem with which I concluded chapter 4, takes its structure from the contrast between here (inland) and there ("deep Eternity," which is "to sea"). This early (1859) examination of the subject uses geographical positioning as metaphor. The soul takes a journey, "out from land": "Past the houses–past the headlands–." The journey, "the going," is an emotional event: it is "Exultation." Eternity is the sea which surrounds the inland soul. ("I cannot tell how Eternity seems. It sweeps around me like a sea," writes Dickinson to Louise and Frances Norcross in 1882.)[6] Just getting to the water is equivalent to "divine intoxication." What happens as one sails onto that sea is not discussed, here. This poem is primarily concerned with using the journey metaphor to make the equation between delight and the suspension of time.

A more complex poem seems to start where poem 76 leaves off, with a closer look at that sea itself.

> As if the Sea should part
> And show a further Sea –
> And that – a further – and the Three
> But a presumption be –
>
> Of Periods of Seas –
> Unvisited of Shores –

Themselves the Verge of Seas to be –
Eternity – is Those –

[695]

To chart the dimensions of eternity Dickinson begins with a spatial vocabulary of seas and shores. To reach eternity, for it takes journeying to get there, one must proceed through not one but a series of seas that part like the paradigmatic red one, each opening upon the next. Yet the key words in this poem are as much *as if, presumption, to be,* as they are *sea* and *shore.* These phrases, which have to do with the act of thinking itself, do more in the poem than show that these seas and shores exist in a mental setting. They indicate that the very existence of eternity is dependent upon them, upon the mind. They are words of supposition, of hypothesis, of the subjunctive, that aspect of language which is "contrary to fact," as the grammar books used to tell us, dealing with acts that cannot take place in the external world.

The poem opens by taking the subjunctive stance. Not "when the seas part," but "As if the seas should part." If one were to imagine a sea parting, showing a more distant sea, and that one parting to show a still further sea; and then, if one were to imagine these three seas as a presumption (a belief not based upon known fact) of periods of seas (that is, cycles of them) and shores no one has ever seen; and if one were to imagine these entirely hypothetical galaxies of seas which by this point in the poem are stretching to the edges of edges only imagined, as themselves the edges of seas that might be, may be—that is eternity. Eternity as idea, existing at the furthest reaches of thought. Eternity is created, as this poem does it, by the mind's ability to think, to imagine, to hypothesize. You reach eternity, as "Exultation is the going / Of an inland soul to sea" also indicates, when you reach past that aspect of mind which reifies body, self, and world to an experience of pure thought, pure idea, pure concept.

Yet to understand, and embrace, speculation is not an easy gesture, when one is as eager as Dickinson is to *know.* I have paired the following poems to show several ways to approach speculation.

Their Height in Heaven comforts not –
Their Glory – nought to me –
'Twas best imperfect – as it was –
I'm finite – I can't see –

The House of Supposition—
The Glimmering Frontier that
Skirts the Acres of Perhaps—
To Me—shows insecure—

The Wealth I had—contented me—
If 'twas a meaner size—
Then I had counted it until
It pleased my narrow Eyes—

Better than larger values—
That show however true—
This timid life of Evidence
Keeps pleading—"I don't know."

[696]

What we see we know somewhat
Be it but a little—
What we don't surmise we do
Though it shows so fickle

I shall vote for Lands with Locks
Granted I can pick 'em—
Transport's doubtful Dividend
Patented by Adam.

[1195]

The first poem (696) was written in the same years as "As if the Sea should part" (695) and placed in the same packet of poems. It casts its vote for "This timid life of Evidence" against "The House of Supposition." Nevertheless, upon further examination we can see that it is really in the same camp as well as fascicle, because its central argument is for personal experience against public doctrine, so that "supposition" here means promises that masquerade as truth with nothing actually to support them.

In poem 696 Dickinson is directly confronting the Christian myth of heaven. The "House" that is called "Possibility" is heaven; its residents are the dead, whose height, glory, and perfection are, after all, a matter of conjecture only. "I'm finite—I can't see—," speaks up the little pragmatist, and we are reminded of the "naive" child in "The Emperor's New Clothes," the only one who "can't see" the fine clothes, which of course aren't there: he *can* see, really.

It is useful to distinguish this "House of Supposition" from poem 657's house of "Possibility." Both are words describing the gestures of the mind, but a crucial distinction is that the latter is where the speaker dwells, and in the former live the dead. Poetry is the "House" of "Possibility," that "fairer house than Prose." It is the here and now of the imagination; it is not in the future, and it is not death. The "Supposition" in this poem is not the speaker's own creation but the projection of others that has been offered to her.

Here geographical analogy is used ironically. It does not help the speaker locate what she seeks, and it is inadequate beside the abstractions she finds. "Possibility" may be equivalent to a "Glittering Frontier," an edge, a transition, but what spreads on the other side are "the Acres of Perhaps." Something more, not less, vague than the frontier itself. It is an understatement to call all this "insecure."

Dickinson is attacking outright Christianity's assurance of a truth founded on nothing empirical, nothing known, by contrasting it to knowledge gleaned from personal experience. "The Wealth I had" is her life. Dickinson labels it meaner, her eyes narrow, but again irony is manifest. If you compare "meaner size" with "Acres of Perhaps," or with their equivalent from stanza four, "larger values," you might well just prefer meaner, though this is against traditional teachings, if it "show." "Narrow eyes" may be smaller, in relation to those acres, they may be blinder ("I'm finite—I can't see—"), unable to "see" all the larger values and glory that are identified, nevertheless, with death. But they are also greedy, especially in this metaphorical context, which presents a person counting her money, her wealth, her life's accumulation. Once again irony sharply undercuts the adjective "timid" with which she prefaces "life of Evidence," as well as the verb "pleading," with which she articulates her radical position, based squarely as it is upon the evidence her mind does have: "I don't know."

One aspect of the poem that creates a tension more than theological is its dramatic situation. Where *is* this speaker? From some uses of the past tense that contrast suddenly with the poem's predominant present tense—" 'Twas best imperfect—as it was—" and "The Wealth I had—contented me"—we might determine that this speaker is herself close upon the "Glimmering Frontier," attempting to hang on to the life of evidence rather than to enter, as she may well be about to do, the unseen and unknown house of supposition. If so, this poem is situated at the very point of crisis to which Dickinson pushes her speakers in the conclusion to "I heard a Fly buzz—when I died—" (465), when she "could not see to see—," or in the conclusion to "I felt

a Funeral, in my Brain" (280), when she "Finished knowing–then–."
One reason for Dickinson's taking this heretical position against a
most basic Christian doctrine, that of heaven, the life after death, is
because, try as she might to know, to experience it with the power of
her imagination, it remains unavailable to her, now. What good is
supposition (somebody else's, at that), when it is presented as fact?

The second poem, 1195, again discusses the conflict between
empiricism and supposition, but this time supposition's daring, even
criminal, procedure is the subject. Here the two positions are expressed as the knowledge that derives from "What we see" ("Be it but
a little") and surmise, what we will do when we don't "see," even
though "it," the object of our speculation, is admittedly difficult to
discern. The word in the first poem for this difficulty was "insecure":
here it is "fickle."

Two analogues complement stanza one, adding evaluation and a
course of action to the original aphoristic observation. The first is, "I
shall vote for Lands with Locks / Granted I can pick 'em –." That this
sentence *is* an analogy is initially more evident from its position than
from what it says, but the fact of that position can help us to arrive at
its meaning. Then "Lands with Locks" becomes equivalent to "What
we see" (which is the "timid life of Evidence"). Land is physical, concrete, and locks keep it contained and definite, all that "Acres of
Perhaps" are not. Yet these locks are allowable only if she can pick
them. The vote here is not exactly for empirical knowledge, not once
those locks are picked. It is rare for Dickinson to be conservative. In
"Their Height in Heaven comforts not" her apparently cautious
stance turns out to be doctrinal rebellion. Here, coming at the topic
from another tack, she reveals her need for daring, even crime. Locks
broken, the land might well grow fickle in configuration, lead the lock
picker straight into surmise. But it would be her own choice, and her
own surmise.

This is her connection with Adam, as the second of the two analogues implies. The linguistic directions that parallelism provides are
at times frustratingly general. Here, for example, it is not immediately apparent to *what* "Transport's doubtful Dividend / Patented
by Adam" is parallel: the couplet that precedes it in stanza two, the
lands with their locks; or stanza one, lines three and four, describing
surmise; or the whole stanza, explaining two kinds of knowing. The
only way to tell is to interpret the cryptic phrase itself, then see.

"Transport" means ecstasy; it also means something carried. No ecstasy without a journey, without crossing through the locks, onto acres (or seas) of speculation. What Adam did was fall, into sin and mortality, but he did so by attempting to transport himself from other limitations, imposed on him by God, limitations of knowledge. His punishment or reward, depending upon how you look at it, his "Dividend," now shared by the human race, is "doubtful." I think that we can read "Transport's doubtful Dividend" as object, like "lands with Locks," of "vote for." I think that the poem expresses Dickinson's support of Adam's sort of lock-picking, speculative thinking, surmise—as long as it is her own crime.

Dickinson votes against the kind of speculation that Christian myth represents, preferring at all times knowledge gleaned from her own experience, be it of body or of mind. Yet another way to deal with the problem raised by that myth is to try, through will and intelligence, to force from it verifiable data.

> To know just how He suffered—would be dear—
> To know if any Human eyes were near
> To whom He could entrust His wavering gaze—
> Until it settled broad—on Paradise—
>
> To know if He was patient—part content—
> Was Dying as He thought—or different—
> Was it a pleasant Day to die—
> And did the Sunshine face His way—
>
> What was His furthest mind—Of Home—or God—
> Or what the Distant say—
> At news that He ceased Human Nature
> Such a Day—
>
> And Wishes—Had He Any—
> Just His Sigh—Accented—
> Had been legible—to Me—
> And was he Confident until
> Ill fluttered out—in Everlasting Well—
>
> And if He spoke—What name was Best—
> What last
> What One broke off with
> At the Drowsiest—
>
> Was He afraid—or tranquil—
> Might He know

How Conscious Consciousness – could grow –
Till Love that was – and Love too best to be –
Meet – and the Junction be Eternity

[622]

The scene, of course, is the paradigmatic death, and resurrection: Christ's. It is supposed to prove the existence of Heaven. And yet is there not a flaw in the logic? Christ may have been human for the duration of his earthly stay, but only a god could have made his decision in the first place. Paradise was never really not of the option for him. Dickinson's efforts to work on that problem, which leads to her perception of the disjunction between Christian myth and ordinary experience, are manifest in her method of attack. She tries to humanize Christ, asking to know the quotidian facts of his experience. "To know," she announces at the outset of the poem, "would be dear –." "Dear" would domesticate, personalize, bring the experience into human perspective.

The series of questions comprising the body of the poem are essentially the same question. Each asks for knowledge of Christ's human response to his dying; each treats him as if he were a subject available for understanding on these terms. The questions seek to know his sensations, thoughts, emotions. Yet as they accumulate in a sequence less developmental than incremental, the humanizing of the experience is all the providence of the speaker. It happens in her questions—"And did the Sunshine face his way"—and not in the answers, which never come. Consequently, the poem comes around, because of its own activities, to embracing speculation as knowledge, the most appropriate way of knowledge for such a situation when one wants to know about eternity.

The first stanza tries to establish the reliability of human dimensions; the vagueness, and vastness, of eternity. The speaker hopes that human eyes were near as Christ died, for there he could "entrust" his gaze; whereas that same gaze, encountering Paradise, would settle "broad."

As a human dying, Christ need *not* be confident or peaceful. This is Dickinson's strategy for using his experience (past) to help her understand her own (future). "Was Dying as He thought – or different –"? From the ambiguity of the question one cannot tell whether he expected pleasure, so that "different" would mean pain, or vice versa. A series of other questions cluster around this issue: "if He was

patient – past content –;" "And was he Confident"; "Was He afraid –
or tranquil –." Try as she does to create, to fill in the situation, these
questions balance their possibilities and do not resolve them.

For example, the possibility that life is to be preferred is raised,
when the speaker asks, "And did the Sunshine face His way –?" That
is, after literal weather was lost to him, did spiritual weather compen-
sate? The possibility of heaven being hellish is also raised: "was he
Confident until / Ill fluttered out – in Everlasting Well –."

Yet at times the speaker cannot maintain her fiction of Christ's
humanity. The progression in stanza three, which queries the subject
of his dying thoughts, "His furthest mind," moves from the human,
"Home," to the divine, "God," to the very myth that he is in the act of
creating: "what the Distant say – / At news that He ceased Human
Nature / Such a Day –."

In this rather random fashion, the poem arrives at its conclusion,
which attempts a resolution of what can only be characterized as
growing confusion. The final lines focus, finally, on knowing itself,
the word which begins the poem and its real subject. For throughout
the poem the speaker has wanted to know what her protagonist knew.
Yet these lines are introduced by the subjunctive, "Might he know."
What they offer, at last, is speculation, not evidence, that the widening
of consciousness, the poem's methodology if not its results, is what
might reconcile or connect the dichotomies that the poem has set up
between this world and eternity. And "Might" seems as much a wish
as a supposition. If consciousness were to grow conscious enough,
then "Love that Was" (love experienced in the human world, the
world of life) and "Love too best to be" (the idea of love) might meet.
This would be eternity, she hopes, when consciousness is not killed
but expanded.

Although its final lines articulate a paradigm for eternity in which
Dickinson wishes to believe, which is not the traditional scenario in
which Christ has the leading role (in attempting to personalize him,
she has made of him more a version of herself than of God), the poem
as a whole fails at its expressed goals. It asks the questions but gets no
answers. It hardly develops but proceeds with some confusion of
structure. At every point the quest for information is foiled: what
remains is speculation. Thus speculation itself persists as the best
form of knowledge for this situation: at any rate, the only one we
have.

The following poem, written about fifteen years later, seems to be a gloss, and a much more successful revision, of "To know just how He suffered –."

Of Paradise' existence
All we know
Is the uncertain certainty –
But its vicinity infer,
By its Bisecting
Messenger –

[1411]

Again the issue is not only the existence but the location of eternity, and the means of approach is, again, emphatically, knowing. What we know, "All we know," is identified in the aphoristic first three lines as the "uncertain certainty." The oxymoron is startling: oughtn't it to be reversed, to read "certain uncertainty"—that is, the knowledge that these matters will always be uncertain? No, because Dickinson is up to something else, something more, here. But what is "uncertain certainty?"

The first three lines, as aphorism, are characteristically abstract, with their vocabulary of *existence, uncertain, certain.* The next three lines move towards embodiment. Their concern is location ("vicinity"); they describe, although abbreviatedly, an action ("Bisecting"), and an agent ("Messenger"). They can be seen to function analogically, giving us an example of "Paradise' existence" and of "uncertain certainty." They provide something of an image, yet at the same time they replace "know" with "infer."

Weisbuch identifies the bisecting messenger as death. "The 'Bisecting Messenger,' death, blocks knowledge but spurs inference," he writes, for "analogy, the language of surmise, can replace certitude."[7] He is probably correct about death, in that Dickinson persistently seeks in that crucial moment its association with eternity; yet here the lack of a specified reference for her metaphor is surely relevant. In the search for location what guidelines we can establish are aided by the appearance of a messenger (from out of its there to our here) which bisects—crosses, divides—our present situation. It creates an experience that radically encounters our present tense (bisecting it) to make us aware of the existence of something else. Located exactly where we cannot say, but that it is located we can infer from the sign of its presence among us, now.

These last three lines function as the kind of analogy to which Weisbuch is referring when he speaks of analogy replacing certitude. Analogy provides data of a different sort from the information of history or science, the impossible answers to the questions asked in "To know just how He suffered –." Its facts are true ones, but they are created within, by the imagination. Hence, analogy *replaces* (Weisbuch's word) certitude; it functions as another way of knowing. In this poem the final three lines parallel and offer an example of the first three lines: they show one way of knowing about "Paradise' existence." In doing so they create an uncertain certainty, which is a definition of speculation as a form of knowledge. Just so the poem replaces the word "know" with "infer." Speculation is a kind of knowing which must include uncertainty in its aptness.

Speculation as a way of knowing, then, is a mental act. It is articulated best by procedures of poetry, such as analogy, which, while they provide concrete forms for conceptual issues, do so on the basis of imagined "facts." The concrete forms are necessary, because the question is location; but empirical data produce the wrong ideas about location, as the following poem explains.

> We pray – to Heaven –
> We prate – of Heaven –
> Relate – when Neighbors die –
> At what o'clock to Heaven – they fled –
> Who saw them – Wherefore fly?
>
> Is Heaven a Place – a Sky – a Tree?
> Location's narrow way is for Ourselves –
> Unto the Dead
> There's no Geography –
>
> But State – Endowal – Focus –
> Where – Omnipresence – fly?
>
> [489]

Ways of location are at issue here. The poem does not negate location itself but contrasts a "narrow" understanding of it with what would be, consequently, a wider way.

The poem's first stanza clearly derides both religion and science as ways for comprehending heaven. (In this poem, heaven is situated temporally, after death.) Both religion's supplication and dogma (praying and prating) and science's search for empirical data ("At what o'clock") lead to the attitude that heaven is literally there and, in consequence, to an inadequate and misleading language for talking about it. "Who saw them" mocks the notion that the transit between life and death can be watched; "Wherefore fly?" reveals the words of flight as silly euphemisms, even as it questions the nature of the destination.

The question introducing stanza two drives home this idea as it exposes the implications of our traditional attitudes with a series of literal locations that become increasingly ludicrous to envision: place, sky, tree? This way of location is much too narrow, dependent as it is upon "geography," terrestrial science, a method of charting literal territory. In matters of the spirit such a word should be seen as metaphor. And if we cannot understand its analogical function, we had best, this poem indicates, forget it.

Location for the dead is better expressed with words like "State," "Endowal," "Focus." These abstractions parallel "Place," "Sky," and "Tree," correcting them. Like the first list, these words are not synonyms; they accrue developmentally. "State" parallels "Place": the latter is physical, the former conceptual—two versions of condition. The relationship between "Endowal" and "Sky" is less self-evident. Endowal, the state of being endowed or provided with, expands the concept of condition to include privilege or asset. Is this "Sky" abtracted? Yes, if sky is the simplistic location for heaven, whereas endowal is the meaning of being there. "Focus" parallels "Tree." Sky is expansive place, and tree, as well as being where birds instead of angels perch, is place contracted, even as focus provides a locus, a central point for state and endowal. Heaven, at once center and circumference, becomes the fitting location for "Omnipresence," which is the soul's condition. A location that is more conceptual than it is physical, thus defined here with abstract rather than concrete words. Metaphor's kind of concrete becomes suspect, because it can all too readily function literally rather than figuratively in traditional patterns of thought and language. This is a blunder, as Dickinson comments in another poem concerned with the problem of language, especially metaphor, and locating eternity: a blunder "in estimate."

> The Blunder is in estimate.
> Eternity is there
> We say, as of a Station –
> Meanwhile he is so near
> He joins me in my Ramble –

Divides abode with me –
No Friend have I that so persists
As this Eternity.

[1684]

"Estimate" is at once a matter of judgment and of proportional relationship. Dickinson's criticism of our clichés for talking about eternity both proposes another set of terms, based on another perception of distances involved, and calls attention to the analogical function, too frequently forgotten, of all these words. Only if we take literally the traditional metaphor of life's process as a journey can we think of eternity as a specific and scheduled stopping-place along its route, "a Station." But Dickinson, pointing out our faulty language habits—"we say"—asks us to consider both a different location and a different way of perceiving location. Not "there" but "near," she rhymes. "There" and "near" are not analogical; they are literal. But they are also abstract. When distance is located and position established literally, the appropriate form is at once proportional and psychological.

When Dickinson substitutes an analogy to create concrete form for her experience of nearness, she personifies place as person, a "he" who walks with her, lives with her. Because eternity is in fact, more than near: it is "so near"; it "so persists." Eternity is personified, because it is experienced as being within her consciousness, within herself. The "he" may be generic, or it may represent another side of herself; but the main point here seems to be that one important way to express what is inner is with, not vocabulary of place, but analogy to self. That all of this is figurative, speculative language is indicated not only by the ways in which this poem calls attention to the language act itself (the capitalization of "Ramble," "Friend," and even "Eternity" seems to have the function of italics here), but by the way the poem contrasts the abstract literal of "there," "near," with its two examples of analogy.

Two prose passages question, as does the preceding poem, the central metaphor of the journey itself, even as they likewise point to eternity's position within the self. "Paradise is no Journey," Dickinson writes in a prose fragment, "because if (he) is within – but for that very cause though – it is the most Arduous of Journeys – because as the Servant Conscientiously says at the Door We are (always – invariably –) out –." "Sweet Sue," she writes to Sue Dickinson in about 1864,

"There is no first, or last, in Forever – It is Centre, there, all the time –
To believe – is enough, and the right of supposing –."[8]

I have said that Dickinson "questions" the journey metaphor, and
this is only partially accurate. She questions its conventionality, and its
literalness. But she goes on to counter it with the same word, "Journey." She is correcting direction, location, and the uses (or loss of)
figuration. If Paradise were located out there and far away, then the
move towards it would be in some sense quite literally a journey. But
if Paradise is all the time within, then the move towards it is a
figurative journey. The most arduous kind, however, because, as a
conceit personifying internal elements enigmatically suggests, we, the
self, are not generally in a condition to partake of its presence. Just
because eternity is located within the mind does not mean that it is
easily or readily accessible.

In the second fragment, Dickinson conflates dimension and temporality by locating eternity not only within but at the center. Always,
how we get there is of supreme importance. There is belief, and there
is also the crucial act of supposition: the stretch, or "journey," of
thought, that encounters the imagination's farthest/innermost places
with the aid of language's power to give concrete form to the ineluct-
ably abstract.

Dickinson's scrutiny of the journey metaphor in these several
places helps in interpreting the following poem.

> The Road to Paradise is plain,
> And holds scarce one.
> Not that it is not firm
> But we presume
> A Dimpled Road
> Is more preferred.
> The Belles of Paradise are few –
> Not me – nor you –
> But unsuspected things –
> Mines have no Wings.
>
> [1491]

Also helpful are the poem's variants. The version quoted is incor-
porated in a letter written to Mrs. Holland on July 4, 1880. In the
second line "just" is erased and "scarce" substituted. Clearly Dickinson's point is that the progress is personal and to be enacted alone.
Another fair copy of the poem, written at about the same time, is

variant in lines three, five, and seven: "Not that it has not room"; "A florid road"; and "The Guests of Paradise are few –." Finally a third version (reproduced in *Bolts of Melody*) derives from a transcript made by Mabel Loomis Todd of a copy presumably now lost. It is variant in line five, where it replaces "florid" with "dappled."

The second verse sentence (lines three through six) once again corrects the doctrinal and simplistic interpretation of the way to paradise. Earth and belief have a literal firmness that is reinforced by "room" and that goes with the concreteness of all the adjectives considered: "Dimpled," "florid," "dappled." But "firm" can also mean actual and can then be understood as a contrast with the more populated, popular, accessible road travelled by belles with dimples, good women who will turn into angels with pretty wings. "Firm" has as well connotations of rigor and purpose (stereotypically masculine) that make it a fit contrast for the stereotypically feminine mode of dimpled belles. Dickinson makes her way, and her understanding, unconventional, special, distinct.

The real road to paradise, plain, lonely, and firm, is also enclosed, deep, interior. It is like a mine; therefore neither a flight nor flighty. Paradise is not analogous to the earth's society—no belles nor guests. Not, I would interpret, "me" or "you" as we are known in society, but "unsuspected things."

Unsuspected things" reminds us that this paradise, this mine, is unknown until experienced, so that the poem's final, summarizing analogy, "Mines have no Wings," stands in the poem as corrective figure to the traditional images for paradise. It may be concrete, but its source is supposition, and its facts are ones found in the imagination. Again, analogy functions properly, as the poem concludes, as the linguistic embodiment of speculation. This way of knowledge, emphatically figurative, is what brings Dickinson closest to ascertaining the location of eternity.

2

The "uncertain certainty" of speculation is a way of locating eternity that finds its sources in the mind's ability to imagine the profoundly unknown and to bring it to embodiment with figurative language, especially, analogy. The poems about speculation as procedure are theoretical in nature. They correspond to those poems I have described in the chapters on pain and delight, poems of concept, of prescription, that precede the event at issue. Even in these poems the problem of language is central, because their subject, eternity, is that moment in the mind when pure abstraction is experienced, when one enters the infinite. Speculation imagines concrete forms, one way to deal with the inherent difficulty of locating (concrete) the infinite (abstract).

None of Dickinson's poems about eternity enact the *media res* that I have discussed in previous chapters. This would be impossible, for the moment of eternity is beyond language. Yet there are poems that come to eternity from the past tense of something that has been experienced. Frequently in these poems there are metaphors where abstract and concrete are juxtaposed so violently that the result is closer to collision than enlightenment. They reflect, I think, what is happening in the mind during eternity's brief moments, where the "dimensional" and "conceptual" aspects of the mind conflate. Sharon Cameron is talking about these metaphors when she writes: "we note that these lines strain toward conceptual realization that will replace, as by an effort of mind, what is visible with depictions that more adequately represent the landscape of the mind."[9] These metaphors create forms that cannot really be imaged but which nonetheless or because of this fact do create awareness of the experience of eternity.

The following poem is a useful place to begin because, while it remains prescriptive and theoretical, it explains but does not undergo this phenomenon.

> Forever – is composed of Nows –
> 'Tis not a different time –
> Except for Infiniteness –
> And Latitude of Home –
>
> From this – experienced Here –
> Remove the Dates – to These –
> Let Months dissolve in further Months –
> And Years – exhale in Years –
>
> Without Debate – or Pause –
> Or Celebrated Days –
> No different Our Years would be
> From Anno Domini's –
>
> [624]

The process described is a progressive abstracting reminiscent of

"As if the Sea should part—" (695). An endlessly extended present is not a new kind of time, but it is time expanded, deepened as much as widened by a release that incurs profoundness. The juxtaposition of "Infiniteness" and "Latitude of Home" shows both expansion and centeredness: deep and wide as versions of one another, both as versions of *home*. (We are reminded of Dickinson's words to Sue Gilbert: "There is no first, or last, in Forever—it is Centre, there, all the time—.")

The remainder of the poem adds detail to its basic proposition. Parallel analogies explain a distinction in the quality of time, time that is conceived of spatially. From "this" to "These" is a movement of abstracting ("Remove the Dates"), even as the dissolving of months into further (or "other," as a different version reads) months, the exhaling of years into years, widens circumference but does not alter identity. Dissolve and exhale, especially, are words that show the imperceptibility and the integrity of the changing.

Again, what creates Anno Domini's years, or calendar years, are debate (in another version, "Certificate"), pause, and celebration. These are some of society's ways of marking meaning, with ritual and social systems like law and education. Society, and the concrete verification of its marking systems, become superfluous when time and space have been internalized somewhere in the mind, which persists as "Home."

The next three poems look back upon an eternity that has been experienced in life.

The first I have discussed before, as a poem that reveals the mind's potential for total expansion. It works to give concrete form to pure abstractness with an hyperbolic and "outer-spatial" vocabulary. The movement in this poem is precisely one from a space experienced as so concrete and so enclosed that the person feels herself bandaged, entirely unable to see, to total insight or vision, which is abstract. Although eternity is not named here, the location to which the speaker comes could be no other place. And yet, as we have learned to expect, the "movement" is entirely mental and happens within what is really only one place, the mind.

> I saw no Way—The Heavens were stitched—
> I felt the Columns close—
> The Earth reversed her Hemispheres—
> I touched the Universe—

And back it slid – and I alone –
A Speck upon a Ball –
Went out upon Circumference –
Beyond the Dip of Bell –

[378]

At first glance my claim for abstractness may appear question-able, since the movement that the poem describes, and its vocabulary for doing so, are entirely tangible: "Heavens," "stitched," "Columns," "Earth," "reversed," "Hemispheres," "touched," "slid," "Speck," "Ball." Yet not only does the quality of the analogical language alter as the transition takes place—it becomes more and more exaggerated— but certain words connected with the final state that the speaker reaches present what amounts to a fiction of concreteness. "Un-iverse," "Circumference," and "the Dip of Bell" are placed in a lin-guistic context that acts as if they were concrete when they are really not.

As the poem begins the speaker is placed in a claustrophobically enclosed setting. She cannot see (a path or route or way); she is inside the heavens, and they are stitched up. In fact, she feels the "columns" (what is supporting the heavens, we assume) not merely standing still but moving in upon her, shutting her in more utterly. Suddenly the situation alters, yet the transition is described as occurring within the same setting. The speaker is not transported but transformed. She is in the same place, but the place has turned inside out, so that stitched heavens are now "the Universe."

But the process is not yet complete. The second stanza moves the speaker further out, to a place rather like the "Forever" of poem 624, where months have dissolved into further months and years have exhaled into years. Dickinson often uses analogy to structures like Chinese boxes or funhouse mirrors, except that the movement de-scribed is that of the same thing forever opening out upon itself rather than reducing itself inward. Having touched the universe is here not sufficient. For it slides further "back," and she goes with it; so that in the final moment of the poem she is very small upon utter enormity at the edge of the circle, or ball. What, where, is the "Dip of Bell"? As curve of a metaphoric bell, or perhaps the arc described by a swinging bell, it may be understood as both sound and shape, the edge of dimension. But in the last line she is not even upon but beyond it. Where is that? Earlier I have described this experience as where one is when one reaches past that aspect of mind that reifies body, self, and world to an experience of pure thought, pure idea, pure concept. Weisbuch calls "Beyond the Dip of Bell" that place "where syllable grows into silence and the language ends" (p. 177). Yet Dickinson tries to find language that will tell about it, concrete analogies for this situation. But words like "circumference" and "Dip of Bell" cannot be imaged concretely, even though they purport to be about concrete things. However, what seems their failure is as well a certain success, because what results from their very difficulty is the intimation of a moment beyond concreteness but yet there, those "Unvisited of Shores –/ Themselves the Verge of Seas to be –." This is language stretched to its breaking point, which is not confusion but is a finale.

The next poem describes eternity itself and not the movement to it nor the state of the person experiencing it. It is less hyperbolic in tone and diction than "I saw no Way – The Heavens were Stitched –," yet it, too, includes examples of this mortal collision between abstract and concrete.

> Great Streets of silence led away
> To Neighborhoods of Pause –
> Here was no Notice – no Dissent
> No Universe – no Laws –
>
> By Clocks, 'twas Morning, and for Night
> The Bells at Distance called –
> But Epoch had no basis here
> For Period exhaled.
>
> [1159]

The "collision" takes place in the phrases, "Neighborhoods of Pause" and "Period Exhaled." In each case, as before, a situation of profound abstractness is described with a phrase in which the concreteness of the analogue proves untenable. Throughout her poems about mental experience Dickinson will use abstract words as if they were concrete; this adds, habitually, a sense of dimension, of substance, to concept. But there is a difference, although one of progression only, between providing the abstract with concrete dimension and revealing its very abstractness with a concrete word or phrase.

This poem describes eternity with an analogy to a town or com-

munity. The first stanza explains its space; the second, its time. Each
stanza centers upon a phrase that effects a collision between spatial
and temporal as well as between concrete and abstract.

In stanza one there occurs that opening out, or in, movement so
characteristic of Dickinson's examinations of eternity. This is as well a
movement from the abstract rendered concretely to the abstract entirely abstracted. "Great Streets of silence" may be interpreted with
the genitive functioning adjectivally—i.e., silent streets. But it can also
mean, and, given this context, probably does mean, streets made of
silence, or silence as path or thoroughfare, with the genitive functioning nominally. Yet these streets open into "Neighborhoods of Pause."
Here "Pause" can only be nominal, not adjectival. And it is very
difficult to imagine a neighborhood made of pause, or pause as creating a neighborhood. First, because pause is a temporal concept, while
neighborhood is spatial. Also, because while neighborhood is com-
fortingly concrete, the noun pause is entirely abstract.

The rest of the stanza is devoted to explaining the phenomenon.
Silence and pause have in common a negative quality: no noise, no
motion. This negative presence is further defined: there is as well a
lack of notice, dissent, universe, and laws. These apparently diverse
concepts are however paralleled, as if all were somehow members of a
similar category. One quality that they do share is that of social organization. "Universe" may be read as the largest of social units, what
many streets, many neighborhoods create. Notice, as a printed or
written statement of information or warning, implements social behavior. Laws are of course rules which govern social behavior, while
dissent is organized refusal. Pause is, then, an absence of social ritual
and social organization. Yet it is nonetheless there, as Dickinson is
trying to demonstrate by calling it, with metaphor, neighborhoods.

The second stanza focuses on time. Again, its message is that,
even as there are forms of space in eternity that can be figuratively
understood as streets and neighborhoods, so time can be given dimension by fitting it out with clocks and bells. But in such a space
society's time must be understood as figuration; for here, as the final
two lines proclaim, such units of time can have no literalness. Because
(for) "Period exhaled." This is the second of the phrases of "collision."
Period is a division of historical time; it is marked, like day and night,
by recurrence. Yet in this place it has exhaled: breathed out, passed
off as vapor. Although we can understand how such an action would

create a place like neighborhoods of pause, it is, again, quite impossible to imagine periods exhaling, and for much the same reasons as outlined before. While period is temporal, the act of exhaling is spatial; period is abstract, exhaled concrete. In other words, the condition about which Dickinson is talking forces her to the extremes of her own linguistic programs for describing mental space.

The final poem is again one that describes eternity, called here, "Immortality," experienced. This time, however, its location is projected inward, not outward, by the process of analogy. This time it is personified, not objectified. Yet, as we have come to understand, these are versions of the same enterprise.

> Conscious am I in my Chamber,
> Of a shapeless friend –
> He doth not attest by Posture –
> Nor Confirm – by Word –
>
> Neither Place – need I present Him –
> Fitter Courtesy
> Hospitable intuition
> Of His Company –
>
> Presence – is His furthest license –
> Neither He to Me
> Nor Myself to Him – by Accent –
> Forfeit Probity –
>
> Weariness of Him, were quainter
> Than Monotony
> Knew a Particle – of Space's
> Vast Society –
>
> Neither if He visit Other –
> Do He dwell – or Nay – know I –
> But Instinct esteem Him
> Immortality –

[679]

The qualities of the "shapeless friend" make him remarkably like the "place" we have come to identify as eternity. As a friend, "he" possesses none of the attributes of a worldly companion: neither physical form, nor speech, nor social activity. Yet although Dickinson defines his abstract qualities with a series of negations, these imply the existence of comparable positive situations. For example, when she says, "He doth not attest by Posture," she indicates that there is some

form in which he does attest; even as he does, also, confirm. In the
second stanza this contrast is made explicit: the *fitter* courtesy is not
external, societal interaction but internal gesture—"Hospitable intui-
tion." The friend—abstract, internal—is nevertheless there. (Chamber may be meant as metaphor for the mind; or it may be literal and
mean her room: the two places are analogous for where she dwells
alone.)

Having established the actuality of her friend in relation to his
shapelessness, Dickinson goes on to examine his location. For whether
eternity is embodied poetically as a place or as a person, understanding of its location remains the abidingly central issue. The last three
stanzas are ferocious in their attempt to articulate the situation of the
self in relation to a presence within itself that partakes of the ultimate
which is beyond itself. Again, abstract clashes against concrete to reveal the nature of this space.

The first line of stanza three is a case in point. *Presence* and *furthest*
pull, push at one another in contexts both spatial and conceptual.
Furthest means greatest, as in both greatest permission and greatest
freedom, i.e., license. But it is also directional; it points to the idea that
to be closest, nearest is the most extreme, the most excessive of free-
doms. Closest can be furthest, wild can be tame—at any rate in this
particular relationship, between self and shapeless friend. The nearly
mirrorlike nature of their situation is suggested by the remainder of
this tense stanza, which insists, as it balances "He to Me" in line two by
"Myself to Him" in line three, upon the mutuality and integrity ("pro-
bity") of the arrangement.

Syntax is especially complicated in the fourth stanza. I am reading these lines with "Monotony" as the subject of "Knew," so that
weariness of him is being compared to the "quaintness" of the idea
(that: understood) there would be monotony in encountering the
vastness of space and its manifold components. Or, one might read
the sentence with the "Particle" as subject of "Knew," so that wearying
of him becomes a notion even quainter than the idea of a star or an
electron wearying of its outer-spatial "Society." In either case the
subject is the comparability of enclosure and limitlessness, private and
public "society," inner and outer "space" in this particular context or
location. "Quainter" is the rather startling comparative term, a word
which mocks society's notions about what constitutes society by reversing them. The idea that interest resides in variety, that excitement

demands vast spaces, is seen as old-fashioned and picturesque, charming but dated.

The poem has consistently employed comparisons with social rituals to define the nature of the speaker's relationship with eternity. Through repeated use of the comparative degree—"Fitter," "quainter"—Dickinson suggests that social values, such as courtesy and hospitality, are not inapplicable but more applicable to what appears to be their opposite, intimacy and privateness. We have seen other of her poems on this subject make similar distinctions. In "Forever – is composed of Nows –"(624) and again in "Great Streets of silence led away" (1159) eternity is presented as a place where social rituals and social systems do not literally apply, but the idea of society still organizes definition. Those poems point to a place *beyond* community; and so, in its own way, does "Conscious am I in my chamber." Those poems define "furthest"; this poem examines "Presence." But of course these are the same. There are two reasons why society conceived of as ritual and organization becomes inappropriate in eternity. One is because it embodies the concrete, while eternity incarnates the abstract. The other is because eternity, to be experienced, requires the opposite of community: aloneness.

The "shapeless friend" is, after all, itself a metaphor for an aspect of self or mind. Dickinson's propensity for distinguishing between parts of herself warns us of this fact, as well as her description in this poem of the friend. He is, as the final line declares, not a "real" friend at all, but a personified abstraction: he is "Immortality." "Instinct," or her own internal emotional sense, understands this. So that we may interpret the first two lines of the final stanza, "Neither if He visit Other –/ Do He dwell – or Nay – know I –," not as contradicting the tenets of the poem (the idea that this particular friend is characterized by his being private, shapeless, never going out in society) but as asserting that other people may have their own version of such a friend, that immortality is not reserved for herself alone, *but* that each person must encounter it, alone.

What these three poems as a group indicate about the experience of eternity is that although it may happen during, it is located beyond. Analogy, language's best procedure for understanding a situation that exists beyond received data, be it that of science or religion, places eternity at center and periphery, finding useful images in outer space, city planning, and etiquette. The first two vocabularies create a beyond at the edges of consciousness; the last one puts the beyond at its center. Consistently, these poems use the concept of community— the norms of social ritual and organization—as contrast for a state that is populated differently, by one. Differently is a key word here, because in these poems which find their rhetorical basis in the comparative degree, the solitude necessary for eternity is not viewed as other but as another, another kind of society. We recall poem 303, "The Soul selects her own Society –." There the soul is shown choosing for company an unidentified "One," but the opening line is ambiguous enough to mean either the society of another or herself as society—"her own Society –," especially when she is referred to immediately afterward as a "divine Majority." Many of Dickinson's poems about the self divide it into components. This is a way to acknowledge the complexity of consciousness, but it is also a constant recognition that the world of the mind does comprise a version of society. A society beyond society. Beyond is an extreme concept; so, too, is the idea that consciousness or the mind is the place where the ultimate social act, the encounter with eternity, occurs. (Traditionally, eternity is a social vision: heaven is completely populated. As is *her* tradition, Dickinson keeps the words but transforms them.)

These poems also show that beyond is almost unbearably difficult to describe with language. The collision between concrete and abstract, spatial and conceptual, that so frequently occurs in analogies about eternity does produce, through its ultimate lack of imagistic reference, a sense, if not sight, of beyond. If eternity is a place that is also beyond language, then language's best efforts to point the reader in its direction should be looked upon not as failure but as unique achievement.

3

It is not surprising, therefore, that in talking about Dickinson's vision of eternity, I should conclude by looking at some of her poems that have as their subject the mind, poems that study the very essence of consciousness. In doing so I come full circle in this book, which began with her poems about the mind as a place most definitely there, concrete, and ends with her poems about eternity, a place which I have called the ultimate abstraction. Finally, the most important definition of the mind is that it is the place where one can meet eternity.

> The Soul's Superior instants
> Occur to Her – alone –
> When friend – and Earth's occasion
> Have infinite withdrawn –
>
> Or She – Herself – ascended
> To too remote a Height
> For lower Recognition
> Than Her Omnipotent –
>
> This Mortal Abolition
> Is seldom – but as fair
> As Apparition – subject
> To Autocratic Air –
>
> Eternity's disclosure
> To favorites – a few –
> Of the Colossal substance
> Of Immortality

[306]

Here, as in others of her poems attesting to the power of the solitary soul, Dickinson makes herself god-like. This posture may be offputting, or it may be inspiring, but it is essential to our understanding of Dickinson's actual position. Her use of spatial metaphors in this poem shows us why. Her omnipotence is associated with height: specifically, extreme height—a beyond, "too remote a height." Solitude is itself presented in terms that locate it far: "When friend – and Earth's occasion / have infinite withdrawn –." "Infinite" is the key word. In this line it means very far indeed; but the subject, and final word, of the poem is "Immortality," always connected in Dickinson's view, and poetic vocabulary, with the infinite. Certain things withdraw that others may take their place. One "society" for another. The everyday world recedes to an extreme distance, the soul ascends to an extreme distance, this brings about extreme power—and it is here and when, although seldom, that immortality is encountered: immortality, or eternity, being enormous, excessive, extreme. The conceptual is rendered spatially, the mind is created as occupied space, yet the "Colossal substance / Of Immortality" is one of those verbal collisions between concrete ("substance") and abstract ("Immortality") where the subject can be surmised but hardly pictured. "Colossal" magnifies the difficulty, because it points both to size and to significance, thus to concrete and abstract, and because it exaggerates them.

Yet to be god-like means not only an experience of power but, as well, an experience *beyond* ordinary mortality, one that is in fact a "Mortal Abolition." We can call such a moment grace, when mortality is transcended, but we should be aware that it is nevertheless not mortality anymore. Dickinson connects its "fairness" to the super- natural as well as to power, in the difficult phrase, "as fair / As Ap- parition – subject / To Autocratic Air ." That is, the supernatural may be a matter of vision, but it is also and at the same time an encounter, in time, with death.

In a letter to Higginson, Dickinson makes both these points.

> . . . I was thinking, today – as I noticed, that the "Supernatural,"
> was only the Natural, disclosed –
>> Not "Revelation" – 'tis – that waits,
>> But our unfurnished eyes –
> . . . Should you, before this reaches you, experience immortality,
> who will inform me of the Exchange?[10]

If the supernatural is the natural disclosed, it is a matter of seeing properly, of vision that is potential always. She opposes the traditional idea of revelation as heaven, a place to which the passive believer goes, with the notion that eternity is up to the person, who can learn to see it. And yet in the final sentence immortality is also connected with actual death.

For death is the vexing matter that Dickinson's concept of eter- nity in life cannot entirely ignore. "Dear friends," she writes to Mrs. Holland, "We cannot believe for each other. I suppose there are depths in every Consciousness, from which we cannot rescue our- selves – to which none can go with us – which represent to us Mortal- ly – the Adventure of Death – How unspeakably sweet and solemn – that whatever awaits us of Doom or Home, we are mentally perma- nent. 'It is finished' can never be said of us."[11]

Are these words about actual, or psychic, death? The letter was written on the occasion of the (actual) death of the Hollands' friend, William Cullen Bryant, and begins, "We thought you cherished Bry- ant, and spoke of you immediately when we heard his fate – if Immor- tality *be* Fate." Yet the query with which her mention of Bryant's death concludes calls into question the relationship between death and immortality. Are they synonymous, or linked causally? That is, Bryant has two fates, death and immortality. Death may or may not lead to immortality, and immortality may or may not need death in order to happen.

Commenting on this letter, Weisbuch says that "any depth in consciousness whose exploration pains and yet enlarges the persona may be considered a type of dying."[12] This is certainly true, yet in her discussions of pain as death Dickinson distinguishes between those deaths, like despair, that kill consciousness, and those deaths, like anguish, that expand it. Equally, in her discussions of literal or actual death, Dickinson worries whether it is an end to consciousness or *the* link to an ultimately expanded consciousness: eternity, immortality. This particular letter both connects all versions of dying, types of one another ("A major alteration in consciousness *is* death," in Weisbuch's words, "an ending and a beginning; differentiations are irrelevant"[13]), and opts for the continuation of consciousness beyond any grave. "We are mentally permanent" is a powerful statement. In the context of my discussion of eternity, her language here is especially provocative. "Doom or home" rhymes opposing fates, linking them in a relationship as complementary as it is contrary. Pain and pleasure, discomfort and comfort, danger and safety: this is the "Adventure of Death," located at the depths of consciousness, the final future that is perpetually present: "'It is finished' can never be said of us."

Consequently, eternity, even when conceived of as a visionary possibility attainable in life at a moment of completely expanded consciousness, is irrevocably linked to death. Some kind of death is involved in the achievement of that vision: "Mortal Abolition." And one takes the risk, obviously, since, no matter how assiduously Dickinson investigates the experience of death itself in her many poems on the subject, one can never know before entering into it whether any death, be it figurative or literal, is going to turn out to be doom or home, the end of consciousness or its liberation. But whatever the outcome, the adventure must be undertaken alone, when and where "friend – and Earth's occasion / Have infinite withdrawn": in the mind.

In the following poem death is the object of the great adventure, but the adventure itself is the act of knowing, the business of consciousness.

This Consciousness that is aware
Of Neighbors and the Sun
Will be the one aware of Death
And that itself alone

Is traversing the interval
Experience between
And most profound experiment
Appointed unto Men—

How adequate unto itself
Its properties shall be
Itself unto itself and none
Shall make discovery.

Adventure most unto itself
The Soul condemned to be—
Attended by a single Hound
Its own identity.

[822]

This often-discussed poem brings back the travel analogy, and the idea of the self as explorer, with which I began this volume, with its title poem, "Soto! Explore thyself!" High adventure, solitude, and the life of the mind are all integrally connected here as in that little epigram. The need for a society that is separate and a terrain that is different is immediately invoked in the opening stanza with the contrast between its second and fourth lines, between the representatives of the outer world, "Neighbors and the Sun" (community and nature) and the denizen of the inner world, "itself alone."

The subject of the first and second stanzas is "This Consciousness"; the verb that controls both stanzas is "is aware." Of what consciousness is aware makes a series of developing importance: the world, then death, then consciousness's own activities.

Consciousness's activities are described spatially, so that the mind's status as place is insisted upon. In stanza two that space is defined with three parallel phrases: "the interval"; [the] "Experience between"; [the] "most profound experiment / Appointed unto Men." "Interval" and "Experience between," although one is about time taken and the other about its content, make us aware of distance situated between two peripheries, as of course does the subordinate verb controlling each of them, "Is traversing." This space, which is the mind, is located precisely between "Neighbors and the Sun" and "Death." It is none other than life. A "most profound experiment," it is further identified as God's gift and charge to humankind.

Life may be God's "appointment," but it is the self's responsibility, as the third stanza makes clear, especially by its repetition of the word "itself." "Itself unto itself" is a self-enclosed world: itself becomes both creator and created, the god and the human, here.

The several itself's—one and its components—are identified in the final justifiably famous lines as the soul and its identity. It is by understanding and metaphorically separating the complexities of the single self that Dickinson provides the alternative society to "Neighbors and the Sun." "Discovery," "Adventure": she insists not only upon the significance but also upon the excitement of the venture that is living in the mind. Here the analogy is to the hunt, so that the explorer-soul hunts its destiny, death, attended by "a single Hound / its own identity." Without that hound, one could presume, a most beautiful, talented, and prized companion, this self would not be "adequate" for the task set.

The hunt analogue recalls another of Dickinson's poems that I have discussed before and provides a gloss upon it.

> Good to hide, and hear 'em hunt!
> Better, to be found,
> If one care to, that is,
> The Fox fits the Hound—
>
> Good to know, and not tell,
> Best, to know and tell,
> Can one find the rare Ear
> Not too dull—
>
> [842]

The poem is written from the perspective of the hidden fox. Yet the fox and the hound "fit," are related, so that the conclusion of the hunt is when, and only when, the fox decides to join with that other aspect of her/himself, the hound. We might read both as parts of the self, the hound as identity. Then this becomes an entirely interior drama, another escapade occurring within the world of the mind.

Such an interpretation becomes even more appropriate when we relate stanza one to the patently analogous stanza two. Then the "rare Ear" becomes, not some special friend or editor from the outside world (there never really was one, after all) but the self, again, in one of its various aspects or incarnations.

In such poems itself is split into its various selves to indicate the "adequacy" of the society within.

The profound association between consciousness in its complex manifestations, death, and eternity, as elements that must define one another, is nowhere more stunningly articulated than in that difficult late poem which concludes by defining eternity as "Costumeless Consciousness." This epithet draws together in its audacious certitude visions of death, mind, and eternity that are especially Dickinson's.

> Those not live yet
> Who doubt to live again –
> "Again" is of a twice
> But this – is one –
> The Ship beneath the Draw
> Aground – is he?
> Death – so – the Hyphen of the Sea –
> Deep is the Schedule
> Of the Disk to be –
> Costumeless Consciousness –
> That is he –
>
>   [1454]

"A surprising abstraction for immortality," says Charles Anderson of this phrase, without further comment. Likewise, Robert Weisbuch is content to paraphrase it as "The presence of a consciousness which will be revealed fully, costumeless, in death" and to think about it further this way: "Costumeless consciousness to be sure, but what will that mean? It is the very continuity of consciousness which makes its future a miracle and a fearful mystery."[14] The phrase *is* surprising, and although its intent is clear enough—the belief in what Weisbuch refers to as "continuity"—its referent is complex and not especially self-evident. Not only does it, as I have suggested, manifest in the most condensed fashion Dickinson's ideas about the relationship between mind, death, and eternity, but it is the controlling metaphor in this extraordinarily opaque poem.

The original of the poem is signed in pencil, "Easter." It is clearly a meditation upon the resurrection and life beyond death. But it progresses from a Christian platitute to a definition of what such "life" might be that is anything but doctrinal.

And although the opening statement is conventional, expressing the idea that doubting immortality makes life on earth inadequate, the tension that is created between its two "lives" complicates these lines in a way that my paraphrase does not reveal. Life is not life, the lines suggest, without the belief in life everlasting. What life is, then, is further called into question when, in lines three and four, Dickinson worries the conventional phrase, "to live again." It is not only lack of belief in heaven that can diminish life on earth but the traditional belief, itself, that heaven will be another, a second "life." "This—is one—." Not two lives at all but one: no difference, then, between life and death?

"This—is one—" is a defiant albeit matter-of-fact utterance that introduces a series of increasingly difficult analogues, standing in opposition and explanation. After spending much careful attention on each of these phrases, Anderson concludes that rather than trying to treat them as "the elaboration of a single conceit of the soul's voyage," "it seems best to keep them separate here, as she does, however bizarre the sequence may seem." He opts for this approach because, by the time he gets to explicating "Deep is the Schedule / Of the Disk to be—," he has come to believe that "the meaning of her language has been made to wander off into uncharacteristic vagueness, for the moon has no connection with immortality and there are no tides actually in this poem."[15] I would prefer to treat the poem, however, as if these images do belong together, although not as a nicely chronological narrative about the ship of life. One does lead to the next, I think, and they move in the direction of that conflation of abstract and concrete which I have been describing as characteristic of language attempting to handle eternity. All, in turn, are informed by the literal phrase that introduces them, "This—is one—," and by the figurative phrase that concludes them, "Costumeless Consciousness—/ That is he—."

The first of the phrases is likewise literal: "The Ship beneath the Draw / Aground—is he?" Anderson reads "Draw" as the dry bed of a stream: "When a ship is seen from a distance passing through the narrows between two bodies of water . . . it appears to have run aground half-buried in the land."[16] However, I would maintain that the use of "beneath" seems more pertinent to "Draw's" meaning drawbridge. The question could be paraphrased as asking: is a ship passing through a drawbridge aground? No, is of course the answer. It is undergoing a transition from one part of a river to another, but it is the same river, and the same ship. It is the drawbridge which is

analogous, "so," to death, which is in turn "the Hyphen of the Sea." A
drawbridge makes a better hyphen than does a streambed, both
visually and symbolically. An hyphen is both pause and connecting
link, and it works nicely to emphasize the transition than does not,
however, interfere with oneness. And it is imageable, but less so than
is "The Ship Beneath the Draw." It does have as well its linguistic
connotation, which makes the life before and the life beyond words,
ideas.

There is no helpful "so" to explain the connection of the following two lines, "Deep is the Schedule/ Of the Disk to be –," to what has
gone before. But since the poem as a whole proceeds analogically, we
understand this to be a further expression and explanation of the
idea that life before and life beyond are one. Yet this phrase, although
apparently concrete—"Deep" provides a spatial context, "Disk" is an
object, and "Schedule" is some plan that has to be reified—is quite
impossible to image, because it is yet another attempt to express the
purely abstract with a language that will somehow reveal its actuality.
It is not that difficult, however, to paraphrase.[17] "The Disk to be" is
the life beyond, and its "Schedule" is "Deep" because it is determined
in the life before: this is one continuous plan. Even as the sea is a
constant image in Dickinson's poetry for life as it becomes eternity—
we remember the sea into which the inland soul goes in poem 76, as
well as the seas that part to show further seas of poem 695, so "Disk"
recalls "out upon Circumference –/ Beyond the Dip of Bell –" (378)
and the various circular symbols for the place where life and eternity
meet, at the center and edge of the mind. Not only is it unnecessary to
follow a ship – river – sea – tide sequence through these analogous
phrases, but it is inappropriate, because the very degree of literal and
figurative, concrete and abstract elements in the language changes as
the words used touch closer and closer to the essence of what is
eternity. The phrases of collision that Dickinson employs at such moments may be startling, frequently puzzling, but they are not con-
fused, nor are they inaccurate.

"Costumeless Consciousness" modifies the "Disk to be," which I
have identified as eternity. The series of appositional phrases make it
likewise possible that "Costumeless Consciousness" might be modifying "Death," "the hyphen of the Sea," or even "The Ship beneath the
Draw"; possibly even the "this" in the phrase, "this – is one –." The

plethora of possible referents makes sense, however, because it is a
syntactical articulation of the thought that "this—is one": life, death,
eternity. Most important is the declaration that all of this, life, death,
eternity, is a version of consciousness itself. A most particular incarnation of the mind: without costume. What makes the phrase so very
odd and interesting is that, literally, consciousness never had a costume to begin with. Consciousness is an abstraction, so that to remove
its outer trappings would be to remove it still further into what it was
all along, to make extreme or to purify its abstractness. To imagine
consciousness as costumeless is what happens in "As if the Sea should
part / And show a further Sea—" (695), when you reach past that aspect of mind which reifies body, self, and world to an experience of
pure thought, pure idea, pure concept. Life is the reified or costumed
version of consciousness; eternity is the pure state of mind.

> Take all away—
> The only thing worth larceny
> Is left—the Immortality—
>
> [1365]

Dickinson may be fascinated by death, but she does not love it. She
braves its looming presence, she commits crimes against the accepted
values of church and state, on behalf not of death but of life. But not
any life, not life imprisoned, shut up in "Prose." Dickinson loves the
expanded life, the extremest life, the life of the mind (which is articulated by poetry) that can continue forever. This final epigram
both attacks and condones death, turning on its two definitions of
"all": the one conventional, the other radical.

"Take all away" refers to death's work, so that what is being taken
away would appear to be life. (The poem's initial inclusion in an 1876
letter to Higginson recalling the memory of her father, who had died
in June, 1874, suggests this reference.) The opening apostrophe may
be addressed to death itself, or to God, or to whatever force it is that
brings about death.

Yet the act of taking away is then labelled "larceny": for it is theft,
a crime of the highest order to steal life. The so-called natural order
of things is not looked upon benignly here. Because life is "all"—how
dare anything steal it!

In the very attack upon proper Christian acceptance of this situation is embedded a radical answer. "All" is not all; for after the theft, the only thing worth such presumptuousness is, it turns out, left— "the Immortality." The theft, in fact, removes the dross to release the essence, so that "all" is understood to be the costume, and the thing left the pure life, consciousness.

The ultimate importance of the word "all" is its absoluteness, its extremeness. Other kinds of deaths, other sorts of living, may as well be invoked here: the all of life in the external world, for example. Dickinson's gamble is that one all, lost, or renounced, will leave space for another all. One that is more suited to her aspirations.

Yet Dickinson is no mystic. She seeks, and arrives at, now and again, this state she calls eternity not because hers is a course of spiritual purification. Connecting her, as some scholars have done, to various Western and Eastern mysticisms does a disservice to her originality and to her pragmatism. She is trying to live, not to transcend life. She chooses to live in the mind as a solution to the practical problems of her situation and, once there, engages in the kinds of activities best suited to her heartfelt desire for a full life. And eternity represents consciousness at its fullest.

Even as eternity represents mental experience at its most extreme, so Dickinson's language for talking about it also represents an extreme form of her customary procedures for describing mental events. Both the equation of analogy with supposition and the collisions between abstract and concrete vocabularies occurring within these analogies exaggerate and underline the special qualities of Dickinson's poetic strategies.

Language that talks about the mind has to be figurative. The mind, although it is of the world, is yet separate from it. The concreteness of things has an analogous counterpart in mental events, but the pivotal word here is analogy. Analogy can use the words for things to explain the mind's dimensionality. But of course these words are used figuratively: there are no literal seas, or prairies, in the mind. Analogy shows like but also difference between whatever it compares and therefore is essential whenever Dickinson talks about mental experience. It is when she begins to speak, not about emotional events such as pain or delight, but a mental situation that is primarily conceptual in nature, eternity, that her language deals as well with how and why it works. Supposition may be the method for incarnating eternity, but it is also what brings all of Dickinson's analogies for mental experience into being. It is always an act of the imagination that yokes the world and the mind in this way. Figurative language takes its reality, not from external data, but from the creative power of the imagination, or supposition.

The fact that eternity is a mental situation primarily characterized by its conceptual qualities, while other mental events, especially emotions, may be understood as being more "tangible," reminds us that the concrete-abstract axis upon which most of Dickinson's analogies are constructed embodies not only the relationship between world and mind but also the nature of the mind itself, which has both concrete (spatial and temporal) and abstract (intellectual, theoretical) dimensions. Dickinson's active abstractions are the other essential component of her analogies. Early in this book (p. ooo), in discussing her poetic techniques, I describe "a structure based upon the encounter, dramatic and reciprocal, between the dimensional and conceptual vocabularies." The reciprocity is important to remember, because although it is necessary for Dickinson to distinguish between two different elements in mental experience, it is one world, not two, that she is describing. Any given analogy requires both parts of the comparison to make its definition. But the drama is also instructive, reminding us that these encounters between concrete and abstract are active and vivid. When the two vocabularies form analogies, the result is both illuminating and unsettling. They are, after all, so deeply different: abstract is, finally, the not-concrete; and vice versa. Figurative language is so thrilling because it insists at the same time that it is false and that it is true. Its truth is imaginative truth, truth that the mind, not the world, makes, and it is real enough. Yet making figures for the mind itself stretches language's capacities to their maximum, which is what those figures of collision that occur when Dickinson talks about eternity represent. Thinking about thinking, talking about thinking, is perhaps the most challenging of enterprises. It verges at all times perilously close to the silence that waits at the furthest limits of language.

Yet of course, that is what Dickinson's adventures have been all about: going to the limits. Even as she forces consciousness to expand to its fullest, that she might experience eternity within life, *costumeless* consciousness, so her poems about the mind push language to its extremes in order that she might articulate her experiences. For Dickinson's self-appointed task, her vocation, is not only to live the fullest, widest, and deepest life: it is to tell about it. She believes that words grant meaning to experience. The words for the life of the mind become extraordinary, in keeping with nature of mental experience.

VI   *"I'm ceded—I've stopped being Theirs"*

IF HER LIFE in the mind may be viewed as Dickinson's most real life, her best life, how shall we define it? How does it represent her creation of her self, the woman she wanted to be? And what does this life, as distinguished from the one she lived in the outer world, where she was the "myth of Amherst," say to those of us today who strive to create our selves as women?

To characterize her mental biography, let us begin, once again, with the mind as occupied space and the choice to dwell there. The choice of solitude. For of course, what I have been describing throughout this book is Dickinson's *perception* of the mind as a place, so that when I look at its dimensionality, for example, I am finding a way to talk about the particular kind of solitude that Dickinson made for herself. What does this sense of dimension do for her?

I have described the changeable properties of these dimensions, the fact that the mind can be experienced as both small, enclosed, restricted and the absolute opposite: limitless. What seems important for Dickinson is having access to both kinds of space, neither at the expense of the other. The mind is probably the only place that really is both, all the time. For the daring and bravery which we find in Dickinson, the ability to test the limits, results at least in part from the security afforded by this particular space: because, although wider than the universe, it is also smaller than a bedroom. Her architectural metaphors are more than descriptive: they show how much the enclosure matters. Dickinson likes keeping that particular house in order.

171

It gives her a control which can then be extended into grander dimensions, but control—and unchallenged possession—at the center are requisite.

It is true, as I have written earlier, that these very limits can also be terrifying, because they force such close encounters with the self. But it is not confrontation that Dickinson fears: it is loss. The fact that she avoided, for so many years, personal meetings with other people, especially with friends, especially with those she loved, stems primarily, I think, from her knowledge that inevitably, in these situations, she would lose: control of the relationship, possession of the person. Her early letters show so much asking; so little answered. She must have learned early how easy it was for her to be turned away. The often violent confrontations with her own self, on the other hand, are always equal. Dominance and submission, "winning" and "losing" are part of the same process: "We're mutual Monarch" (642). Thus while the domestic world of personal relationships could not be safe for one as intense ("unwomanly"?) as Dickinson, the house of the mind could.

This control and possession at the center, rendered metaphorically with images of house and home, cannot be achieved in the actual presence of other people, so Dickinson believes. Yet because she is not at all "anti-social," her version of living alone (living in the mind) is a peculiarly social one. She populates her inner world with a society of selves. Her many poems about the mind with their social as well as geographic metaphors let us see how necessary it was for her to be in relationship; for that was how, I think, as a woman she could not help but define her humanity. This is a different kind of solitude from that of the person who enjoys being alone.

Dickinson's need for the wider dimensions of the mind is perhaps simpler to understand, because in a patriarchal society we associate journeys and vistas, heights and depths, with conquest and accomplishment. Naturally, we reason, someone who wanted to achieve would need to reach. But of course, Dickinson's metaphors of continents and worlds are figurative, describing experience but not actual lands and skies. Walt Whitman did travel across America, but Emily Dickinson did not. This is a woman's version of discovery, after all. At home if no longer safe.

The mind, then, becomes a place that embodies versions of traditionally female and male territory, while at the same time being unusual in that it is both, and also neither. The enclosed, the private, the personal, the domestic are traditionally woman's space, while the opposite, those vistas, are for men. In this as in so many other ways, society neatly bifurcates the female and the male. Actual women, like actual men, have propensities, in varying degrees, for both. When Emily Dickinson sought to incarnate her actual self, she neither tried to join a male profession, poetry, by being "like a man" (although she also possessed her share of courage and daring), nor did she restrict her gifts to the conventional life of a woman—or, it must be added, to conventional "women's verse." The mind as she understood it was the only environment available to her that could serve her needs both for a world she could control and one that offered her the range within which she could test herself. That she had to choose solitude is essentially a critique, and a revision, of the society in which she lived.

Control and possession are Dickinson's goals, power her achievement, loss her terror, as within the mind she encounters intensest emotion and profoundest thought. Pain, delight, and eternity, as examples of the scope of mental events, provide the experiences through which she develops her capacity for control and possession, her responses to loss, her abilities to be powerful: in other words, this is how she creates her self.

Control and possession are aspects of the kind of strength that Dickinson needs in order to have power. Control is a way of taking possession, or vice versa: possession is keeping what one wants. Power results from control and possession: it is the ability to act, and to act well. If control and possession keep things stable, power sets them in motion, but in accordance with the desires of the one who moves them. Loss, on the other hand, is absence. It renders Dickinson impotent, keeping her from experience, expression, and of course, from power.

First let us look, not at power, but at loss, since I think that Dickinson's lifelong struggle with this debilitating force helped her to develop the special kind of power she did possess. For Dickinson, all loss is some version of the absence of feeling. Not to feel is pointless: it is not to be alive and, therefore, it is death. Thus Dickinson courts all feelings and finds value therein.

Pain, as I have shown, because of its vitality and its pedagogical potential, is worthy of pursuit, even though it admittedly hurts. The danger of pain is not its discomfort (for that, too, is sensation) but that, if it grows too great, either psychologically or physically, it will turn into its opposite, despair or death, lack of all feeling—loss. Delight, because it is pleasure, not pain, leads even more quickly to loss and to losses that are greater. At least pain hurts, so that when it stops, there is some comfort. (Though, to Dickinson's way of thinking, not much.) When delight stops, one is confronted with the double experience that is loss of feeling and loss of a feeling that has been pleasant. But, on the other hand, when delight has not stopped, it consumes the self in its process, because it annihilates both identity and control. (The beauty of pain is that undergoing it can establish control—unless and until it gets too great.) Finally, the danger in seeking eternity, which represents the mind expanded to its fullest conceptual capacity, is yet another kind of loss: actual death.

In the world that Dickinson watches from her window, the world of nature, loss is behind every corner, beneath every bush. The process of time itself, which controls the natural world, is equivalent to loss. And loss, each time it happens, is death: an overwhelming problem when what one most wishes to be is alive, all the time.

Nor is the mind exempt from time's power, since the mind, while it is in important ways unlike nature, is like it, too, as Dickinson's poems demonstrate. Thus time becomes a major opponent of Dickinson's, since it is loss's most active agent. Somehow, time itself must be controlled, if loss is to be battled. And obviously, something must be done with loss to weaken it, to render it, if possible, impotent. Renunciation is the discovery that Dickinson makes, finding a form, as I have pointed out, already available to her in Christian tradition and especially in traditional proscriptions for womanly behavior. In these versions of renunciation, it is a self-sacrifice which, while it is meant to ennoble and strengthen the self, still demands in recompense the loss of whatever it is one wanted. In Dickinson, however, renunciation becomes less a giving up than a transformation.

Renunciation is a way to say no, and as such it puts power suddenly in the hands of the previously powerless. For example, Dickinson's move into the mind may be understood as renunciation, giving up the "normal" life of a woman—lovers, husband, children, and home: but for something else, solitude. Something that while it may seem like an absence, is emphatically a presence, as populated, although differently, as any Amherst quilting bee. Saying no to the conditions that oppress one clears a space, into which one may put— whatever one wants to be there, providing one is strong enough and creative enough. Renunciation becomes a form of rebellion that is not, however, fought on the terms or on the territory of those in power. It is, perhaps, a "slant" revolution. You give up their terms altogether, replace them with your own, when they don't even know that you are doing it.

Thus we may construe Dickinson's move into the mind as a particularly successful version of renunciation. Once there, she found the tactic equally useful for the psychological issues that beset her life; especially, her desire to be most thoroughly alive. As I have described in this book, Dickinson's strategy with loss of delight, of love, was to renounce the delight that caused the loss, thereby clearing a space in which something else might happen. But the something else, as her poems indicate, was a transformation of the same thing, love, delight, into forms that transcend time, grant her control of the situation, possession of the beloved, and therefore are without loss. Dickinson envisions a radical kind of love that denies the basic premises of heterosexual love as we know it in a patriarchal society. Yes, she had to do this in her mind and not in the "real world"; for only in her mind, as she understands the problem, can such a space be cleared. But in that clearing she can create, by means of the imagination, love on her own terms, leading neither to loss of possession (of the beloved), loss of feeling (it lasts), or loss of self (she is in control).

Renunciation may seem to be making a religion of loss, to be hallowing it. On the contrary, it begins by exaggerating the space and condition of loss, creating its pure negation, so that a transformation might occur which is anything but absence. In this way, by possessing them, Dickinson achieves control over her demons. This control, which means an assertion of self, is at the root of her power.

Dickinson's power is the ability to do her best work. This requires the ability to be her best self, live her best life—and then write about it. Conversely, the act of doing her best work is at least partly responsible for creating, as well as describing, that self and that life.

As this book has demonstrated, poetry becomes Dickinson's most effective way for understanding and controlling mental experience. The poems, with their structure of parallelled analogy, measure mental events: locating each with graphs of circumference; charting its relative position in the spatial and temporal dimensions that comprise the mental world. By these procedures Dickinson defines what happens to her. Yet her poems define in a way that is not developmental or logical, perhaps because mental experience is not suited to the kinds of intellectual control that syllogism provides, perhaps because it is not outside the mind but within it. Dickinson's definitions accrue, through the process of apposition. The parallel structure works laterally, not linearly, by the end including all the possibilities, or analogies, that it has established, rather than denying or overcoming some to arrive at a designated conclusion. Such a structure gives Dickinson control, and possession, of her subject, not by appropriating or subsuming it, but by ordering it, arranging it, encircling it: putting herself in a thereby clarified relationship to it. One may sense in these remarks comparisons between "masculine" and "feminine" modes of discourse. Indeed, Margaret Homans has argued eloquently about patriarchal language's appropriative function and has described Dickinson's non-hierarchical uses of language.[1] Dickinson never relinquishes a need for possession and control, but her methodology does indicate that she arrives at and uses these powers differently from what is the traditional masculine style. For my present purposes I do not wish to pursue these comparisons at length but rather to focus on this manner of definition as Dickinson's own. I would not be surprised, however, if it were demonstrated to be a characteristic of her femaleness, a particularly successful form of women's rhetoric. Certainly, it is especially suited to arrange the analogies and metaphors that Dickinson requires in talking about mental experience.

Language's power in articulating mental experience is two-fold. The first I have just discussed: its analytic capacity, here meeting the demands made by the mind's spatial properties. Thus Dickinson, as an "explorer" of mental lands, maps those terrains systematically, with supreme precision of linguistic measurement. The second is language's creative power, the power of the imagination, of supposition or speculation, rendered linguistically through figuration; especially, analogy and metaphor. I have talked at length about why Dickinson needs figure to articulate mental experience, why the mind and the world are comparable but different, so that the bridge analogy makes between world and mind serves to admit the world's vocabulary of the concrete and the tangible into the space of the mind and then adjusts its meaning there. Dickinson is solitary, but she is no solipsist. She does not disavow the existence of the outer world to live within; in fact, she needs its things and events as points of departure, from which to begin her own adventuring. Analogy is so useful because it has at least one "foot" embedded in the state of things as they are. But, to continue this awkward metaphor, the other foot is free to dance. The power of the imagination is its ability to speculate, suppose, create. Metaphor embodies the imagination, calling what is not true in the real world true in a different real world. When Dickinson describes mental experience with language primarily figurative, she is incarnating the mind's ability to create, as much as codify, experience. Experiences like pain, delight, and eternity, as they occur within the mind, no matter what their sources in the external world, are made susceptible to the creative power of the imagination there. Dickinson, undergoing pain or delight, may react and respond to their strong pressures, but also she can strive to make them happen as she wants. Her control of delight is a provocative case in point. Her brilliant figurative language—especially, analogies complicated by metaphor—constantly controls and possesses experience in this way: by creating it. The mind is, after all, just the weight of God, as Dickinson reminds us in poem 632. They differ, if they do, "As Syllable from Sound–." Syllable means language, which can be distinguished from undifferentiated sound in having a form and a shape that people make. But language, as this poem asserts, is agent for the mind's creation and is equal in its function to God.

People have always seen power in Dickinson's poetry. Few would dispute its greatness. But of course, as I have argued before, this poetry was traditionally seen to have little to do with the woman who wrote it, who, if discussed at all, was viewed as anything but powerful: a spinster, a recluse, an eccentric, even a madwoman; peculiar, unnatural, frustrated, deprived, unhappy, unfulfilled. In John Cody's words about her later years: "Loveless, excluded, almost burned out as a poet, and reduced to the status of a queer, hypochondriacal and depressed old maid."[2] In contrast, my argument, like that of other feminist critics, has been that her life informed her work, made her work possible and probable. Further, as I have maintained, Dickinson's most important life was primarily interior but nonetheless real, and I have written this book as a biography of that mental life. Therefore, Dickinson's power rests not only in her work but in the way in which she made it possible for herself to do that work, the way in which she created herself. The way in which she created a solitude that was neither a retreat, nor a prison, nor a vacuum, nor a negation.

"But didn't she want to be happy," my students always ask, notwithstanding their admiration for her exceptional achievement. I usually answer, "Yes; but more important, she wanted to be alive." She could not have both, not in the society that was her birthright.

What about us, I often think. Does Dickinson's example, like that of many talented and ambitious women in her own and other centuries, tell us today that only by giving up the world (that flawed and oppressive patriarchy) can we, as talented and ambitious women, know a world in which we can truly create ourselves? The world of solitude, I mean: the world of the mind. It is surely one path, and Dickinson's life there clearly demonstrates how viable, admirable, successful it can be. But I believe that Dickinson's example has wider applicability. For it tells us something, even if we do not willingly choose solitude, about the power of the creative imagination in respect to women's peculiar problems in a sexist society. We have to create ourselves, because, as we know, the patriarchy is only too willing to do it for us, as it always has, to our disadvantage at the very least, or suppression and oppression at the most. In a recent letter the poet and scholar Josephine Miles speaks of trying "to create something that's yours beyond what others can give," of learning about "the resources of creation."³ Dickinson's life in the mind demonstrates how mental experience can be the source of this creation, despite society's definitions, values, and norms; how what happens within ourselves—in some version or another of a solitude—might seriously affect the self who walks at large.

Yet society is so powerful; out there this new current might well be damaged or cut off. This is what Dickinson believed, and she may have been wiser than any of us knows. She knew she needed some manner of safety, and control, in order to be brave. This safe place is difficult to find in the patriarchal world. It is a great gamble, and we hardly know what success, or how much success, is possible that way. But surely no one who takes Dickinson seriously can ever minimize the power of the imagination, of the mind, in creating the self one would wish to be. Dickinson's discoveries in that hitherto "undiscovered continent" reveal the enormous scope of its possibilities.

NOTES

1. "The Landscape of the Spirit"

1. *The Letters of Emily Dickinson*, 3 vols., ed. Thomas H. Johnson and Theodora Ward (Cambridge: The Belknap Press of Harvard University Press, 1958), II, #315, p. 450.

2. George Whicher, *This Was a Poet* (Ann Arbor: University of Michigan Press, 1938), pp. 139, 272, 113.

3. John Cody, *After Great Pain* (Cambridge: The Belknap Press of Harvard University Press, 1971), pp. 484, 103, 171, 391.

4. David Porter, *Dickinson: The Modern Idiom* (Cambridge, Mass., and London: Harvard University Press, 1981), pp. 114, 121.

5. I have analyzed more copiously the styles of sexism in traditional Dickinson criticism in "'A Privilege So Awful': The Poetry of Emily Dickinson," *Naked and Fiery Forms: Modern American Poetry by Women, A New Tradition* (New York: Harper and Row, 1976), pp. 7–32. I have treated the same subject more recently in my introduction to *Feminist Critics Read Emily Dickinson*, ed. Suzanne Juhasz (Bloomington: Indiana University Press, 1983).

6. Richard Sewall, *The Life of Emily Dickinson*, 2 vols. New York: Farrar, Straus and Giroux, 1974), p. 4.

7. Sandra M. Gilbert and Susan Gubar, *The Madwoman in the Attic: The Woman Writer and the Nineteenth-Century Literary Imagination* (New Haven and London: Yale University Press, 1979); Karl Keller, *The Only Kangaroo Among the Beauty: Emily Dickinson and America* (Baltimore and London: The Johns Hopkins University Press, 1979); Margaret Homans, *Women Writers and Poetic Identity: Dorothy Wordsworth, Emily Brontë, and Emily Dickinson* (Princeton: Princeton University Press, 1980); Joanne Feit Diehl, *Dickinson and the Romantic Imagination* (Princeton: Princeton University Press, 1981); Barbara Antonina Clarke Mossberg, *Emily Dickinson: When a Writer Is a Daughter* (Bloomington: Indiana University Press, 1982.)

8. Juhasz, *Naked and Fiery Forms*, pp. 1–6.

9. *Letters*, I, #31, p. 88.

10. Homans, pp. 166–71.

11. *Letters*, I, #39, p. 104.

12. *Letters*, I, #110, p. 235.

13. *Letters*, II, #261, p. 405; #265, p. 408; #271, p. 415.

14. Cody, p. 55.

15. Gilbert and Gubar, p. 590.

16. *Letters*, I, #39, pp. 104–5.

17. *Letters*, I, #93, p. 210.

18. The essays by Dobson and Morris are in *Feminist Critics Read Emily Dickinson*.

19. Gilbert and Gubar, p. 595.

20. Mossberg, in *Feminist Critics Read Emily Dickinson*, p. 60.

21. Sewall, pp. 517–18.

22. *Letters,* II, #318, p. 452.

23. Porter, pp. 55, 129, 245.

24. Patricia Meyer Spacks, *The Female Imagination* (New York: Alfred Knopf, 1975), pp. 315, 322.

25. Virginia Woolf, *To the Lighthouse* (New York: Harcourt Brace and World, 1955), pp. 95–96.

26. Gilbert and Gubar, p. 48.

27. Homans, p. 12.

28. Diehl, p. 11.

29. Jean Mudge, *Emily Dickinson and the Image of Home* (Amherst: University of Massachusetts Press, 1975).

30. This is Albert Gelpi's definition of circumference from *Emily Dickinson: The Mind of the Poet* (New York: W. W. Norton, 1965), p. 122. In *The Tenth Muse: The Psyche of the American Poet* (Cambridge, Mass., and London: Harvard University Press, 1975) Gelpi further defines circumference as enclosing "the totality of expansible psychic activity." "Dickinson's circles," he observes, are not biological or genital symbols but images of psychological or spiritual space" (p. 271).

2. "To Make a Prairie"

1. Dickinson's use of analogy and an accompanying parallel structure has been noted by many scholars. For example, Carroll Laverty, in a brief article listing structural patterns in Dickinson's poetry, identifies them as "1) statement or presentation of situation followed by explanation or example and sometimes an application of the statement to the theme; 2) parallelism in various forms; 3) statement based on analogy; 4) a logical argument—inductive or deductive development of a thought; 5) statement in the form of definition; 6) dramatic structure; 7) one single statement; and 8) the combination of two or more of the first seven" ("Structural Patterns in Emily Dickinson's Poetry," *Emerson Society Quarterly* No. 44 [1966]: 13). Laverty attributes these patterns to the intellectual process of a mind trying to deal with emotion. Brita Lindberg-Seyersted, in *The Voice of the Poet: Aspects of Style in the Poetry of Emily Dickinson*, comments both on Dickinson's tendency to contrast concrete and abstract and on parallelism as a significant rhetorical pattern in her poems; she notes emphasis as a means of contrasting abstract and concrete; binding as a function of the parallelism (Cambridge: Harvard University Press, 1961, pp. 92–97, 198–204).

By far the most interesting discussion of analogy is Robert Weisbuch's in *Emily Dickinson's Poetry* (Chicago: University of Chicago Press, 1975). "Dickinson's typical poem enacts a hypothesis about the world by patterning a parallel, analogical world," he writes (p. 12), and goes on to discuss in sensible and sensitive detail how analogical progression develops by a series of perceptions or stories. "Each is at least partially analogous to the others and each reveals a new aspect or consequence of putting the world together in the particular, often unstated way which links the otherwise disparate examples" (p. 14). Weisbuch's conclusion is that the poem is, finally, "sceneless," that "mimetic situations are transformed, transported to a world of analogical language which exists in parallel to a world of experience, as its definition" (p. 19). I would argue only that there is a scene, a setting, and that is the mind. The world of the poem is always mimetic of something, is more than simply itself, and here the analogical structure is patterned upon mental structure, the world of the mind.

2. Weisbuch, p. 13.

3. Cristanne Miller, *Terms and Golden Words: Dickinson's Use and Ideas of Language as They Explicate Her Poetry,* Ph.D diss., University of Chicago, 1980, p. 46.

4. Keller, p. 169.

5. Ibid., pp. 169–170.

6. Ibid., p. 180.

7. Sharon Cameron, *Lyric Time: Dickinson and the Limits of the Genre* (Baltimore and London: The Johns Hopkins University Press, 1979), p. 12.

8. *Jane Austen's Letters,* ed. R. W. Chapman (Oxford: The Clarendon Press, 1932), p. 134.

9. *The Works of Anne Bradstreet,* ed. Jeannine Hensley (Cambridge: The Belknap Press of Harvard University Press, 1967), p. 15.

10. Weisbuch, p. 14.

11. Which may be why this poem, well-known, oft-analyzed and usually considered central to Dickinson's attitude toward nature, has given rise to such contradictory interpretations. For Albert Gelpi it shows how "Matter and Spirit, concrete and universal are the same" (*Emily Dickinson: The Mind of the Poet* p. 82). For Charles Anderson, in *Emily Dickinson's Poetry: Stairway of Surprise* (New York: Holt, Rinehart and Winston, 1960), its concluding lines "place ironic limitations on her ability to 'know'": "she is powerless in her limited 'Wisdom' to understand the inner truth of nature, because of its remoteness" (p. 83). For Robert Weisbuch, Dickinson in this poem "stresses cognitive limitations in order to elevate experience, to make the world strange and new again" (p. 68). To these views I can only add my own.

12. Margaret Homans, discussing Dickinson's recognition of the dislocation that exists between words and things, points out that this kind of "explosion" is essential to Dickinson's use of poetic language. "Dickinson's art is not impeded in any way by her recognition that nature is not to be possessed, because she understands and makes use of a general dislocation between words and their referents that includes, but is not limited to, language's relation to nature. Because she knows that all language is figurative, she feels no special distress at the discovery that actual nature is not the same as the words used to name it," she writes. "Emerson," she continues,"even though he shares some of Dickinson's knowledge of the virtiginous freedom of language, is disconcerted by nature's elusiveness, because his views of language include its powerful propriation of nature" (p. 193).

13. Charles Anderson's remarks about this poem comment more historically about Dickinson's use of the word "absolute." He reads the poem similarly but does not go on to talk about ideas.

> Her meaning presumably takes off from Locke's distinction between the primary qualities of objects, which are absolute in the sense that they exist whether perceived or not (such as bulk, extension, and motion), and their secondary qualities, which depend on the perceiver for their existence (such as taste and color). But by adding that the Absolute Object is "nought" she embraces the modern extension of this concept, namely, that since these absolute qualities lie beyond the bounds of

human perception they are as nothing to her. This central negation, then, is not so much a denial of the existence of the material world from the standpoint of traditional Idealism as it is a recognition that in a strict sense it is unknowable by the consciousness, as in the terms of the new theoretical physics, and hence has no graspable meaning for man. He is left in the end with his perceptions. He can only know what he perceives, what he himself "creates." This alone has value or meaning. [p. 91]

3. "Peril as a Possession"

1. Weisbuch, p. 123.

2. Suzanne Juhasz, "Transformations in Feminist Poetry," *Frontiers: A Journal of Women Studies* 4, no. 1 (Spring 1979): 24. The full sentence reads, "There is a universal of the personal, by which sets of particulars—those of writer and reader, for instance—connect, so that truths are established."

3. Sewall, II, p. 618.

4. Anderson, p. 203. Anderson calls this "almost clinical" mode the procedure she adopted "to gain the proper distance between her personal emotions and her art," what saves her from sentimentality. Distance, yes, but, I would argue, less for the sake of objectivity or depersonalization than for control, "possession."

5. Weisbuch, p. 117.

6. Noah Webster, *An American Dictionary of the English Language* (Springfield, Mass.: George and Charles Merriam, 1848), p. 325.

7. Weisbuch, p. 150; Gelpi, *The Tenth Muse*, p. 276; Weisbuch, p. 150.

8. Weisbuch, p. 150.

9. Cameron, p. 49. Cameron argues that the speaker of this poem is "at the center of her subject and hence unable to see its totality," so that "she is often at a loss to know what it is" (p. 49). I think that Dickinson knows full well what it is, and that her complex rhetoric proceeds not from "the failure to understand the workings of one's own mind" (p. 48) but from the systematic search for verbal equivalents for such extreme emotion.

10. Ibid., p. 50.

11. Charles Anderson sees these lines as an image of death in which the body is being carpentered into a coffin, so that coffin and corpse become one (p. 213).

12. Winifred Nowottny, in *The Language Poets Use* (London: The Athlone Press, 1965), discusses the complicated process that is the interpretation of metaphor. Commenting on Stephen Spender's line, "Afternoon burns upon the wires of the sea," she writes: "It involves linguistic inferences as to a *something-of-the-sea* corresponding to *the wires of a harp*—and, when these have been made, a sorting of our own knowledge of sea-structure and our knowledge of harp-structure until we come up with whatever particular aspect of sea best corresponds to harp-wires and best meets all the other specifications given by the utterance we are interpreting. . . . A metaphor is thus a set of linguistic directions for supplying the sense of an unwritten literal term" (p. 59). Consequently, she observes, discussing metaphor and its relation to the world of private emotion," the vocabulary of emotion is comparatively little developed—no doubt because emotions cannot be pointed to and identified

as one can point to and identify shades of color. Metaphor is therefore a useful means of dealing with the area of unnamed experiences" (p. 60).

13. Anderson, p. 215.

14. Cameron, pp. 168-69.

4. "Delight is as the Flight"

1. "Parhelion," according to Dickinson's dictionary, is "a mock sun or meteor, appearing in the form of a bright light near the sun; sometimes tinged with colors like the rainbow, with a luminous train" (Noah Webster, *An American Dictionary of the English Language*, p. 798). There is no way to ascertain with certitude that Dickinson is playing with echoes of the other astronomical term, but the fact that the two words are so close, yet the difference between them is precisely the difference, and confusion, that she is postulating between delight and enchantment in the poem, is intriguing.

2. Anderson, p. 184; Keller, p. 25.

3. For example, as Anderson writes: "The sign and bars could then be heraldic devices acquired by the new nobleman, the royal seal entitling him to wear the ermine of exalted rank" (p. 185). Nevertheless, Anderson is one of the very few who have attempted explication of this strange, "obscure" poem. "The multivalence of all this language sends the mind on far journeys," he remarks (p. 185).

4. Keller, p. 25.

5. Barbara Mossberg, in "Metaphysics of a Yankee Mother Goose," in a lengthy examination of Dickinson's child persona, speaks of her as a "career child," and of the "subversive innocence" that her persona permits: Dickinson uses the rhetoric and tone of the child and the child persona "to affect a certain kind of heretical subversiveness—a safe vantage from which to criticize and fend off an encroaching absurd adult world in which even as an adult she has no power or important role" (*Feminist Critics Read Emily Dickinson*, p. 48). Nina Baym, also discussing Dickinson's use of the child persona, writes: "Dickinson uses the mask of a child both to express a truth and as a strategy to avoid the results of speaking that truth. Knowing herself weak, and expressing the emotions rising from that sense of weakness, she also uses her weakness as a shield. This is a trick both childish and feminine, a trick of the powerless" ("God, Father, and Lover in Dickinson's Poetry," in *Puritan Influences in American Literature*, ed. Emory Elliott. [Urbana, Chicago, London: University of Illinois Press, 1979], p. 199).

6. As argued by Rebecca Patterson in *The Riddle of Emily Dickinson* (Boston and New York: Houghton Mifflin, 1951) and the posthumously published *Emily Dickinson's Imagery* (Amherst: University of Massachusetts Press, 1979), as well as recent feminist critics, such as Lillian Faderman, "Emily Dickinson's Letters to Sue," *Massachusetts Review* 18 (1977): 197-225 and "Who Hid Lesbian History?" *Frontiers: A Journal of Women Studies* 4, no. 3 (Fall 1979): 74-76, and Nadean Bishop, "Renunciation in the Bridal Poems of Emily Dickinson," presented at the National Women's Studies Association Conference, 18 May 1980.

7. When the poem was published in the *Springfield Daily Republican* for 4 May 1861, the final line was altered, editorially, to read, "Come staggering toward the sun." This of course removes entirely the hyperbole, the fantasy, and the meaning.

8. Charles Anderson notices "the struggle between earthly and heavenly love," stating that "the largest successful group of her love poems centers around the ritual of marriage; these also move steadily away from the human institution, which was not a part of her experience, towards several versions of the betrothal in heaven that became an obsessive and perhaps compensatory image with her" (pp. 180, 178). William Sherwood, in *Circumference and Circumstance: Stages in the Mind and Art of Emily Dickinson* (New York and London: Columbia University Press, 1968) finds that "the figure of the bride was used to express that moment when, to recall Perry Miller's felicitous description of grace, 'the finite impinged upon the infinite.' To denote such a moment of communion, commitment, and passage to a higher state, the sacraments of marriage and baptism and the metaphoric actions of the acquirement of riches or of the dawning into everlasting light had traditionally been found to be adequate" (p. 149).

9. The all-encompassing nature of love is underlined in the following epigram:

> Love – is anterior to Life –
> Posterior – to Death –
> Initial of Creation, and
> The Exponent of Earth –
> [917]

10. Erich Auerbach defines figural interpretation, which is a system of analogy, as follows: "Figural interpretation establishes a connection between two events or persons, the first of which signifies not only itself but also the second, while the second encompasses or fulfills the first" ("Figura," in *Scenes from the Drama of European Literature: Six Essays* [New York: Meridian Books, 1959], p. 53).

11. Baym, p. 205.

12. Anderson, pp. 182–83; Cameron, p. 86.

13. Ibid.

14. Ibid.

15. Anderson, p. 183.

16. Ibid.

17. Gilbert and Gubar, pp. 589–90.

18. Ibid., pp. 588–89.

19. Ibid., p. 595.

20. John Todd, *Emily Dickinson's Use of the Persona* (The Hague: Mouton, 1973), p. 19.

21. Patterson, *Emily Dickinson's Imagery*.

22. Keller, p. 68; p. 58; p. 84; p. 64.

23. Gilbert and Gubar, p. 575.

24. Gilbert and Gubar note: "that 'Goblin Market' is not just an observation of the lives of other women but an accurate account of the aesthetics Rossetti worked out for herself helps finally to explain why, although Keats can imagine asserting himself from beyond the grave, Rossetti, banqueting on bitterness, must bury herself alive in a coffin of renunciation" (pp. 574–75).

25. Cameron, p. 153.

26. Cameron, p. 40. Cameron reads persistently through the admittedly "convoluted" syntax of the poem's final lines to discuss how the lines reveal

"several iterations of the concept of self: the sense in which renunciation is an act that violates the self; the sense in which it is an act that legitimates the self; and the sense in which the self stands as ambivalent arbiter between the two" (p. 41). Yet I do not agree with her analysis of the tone of the lines, that of "someone trying to convince herself of something she finds both difficult and imperative to believe—that renunciation is a virtue; that it is piercing she knows" (p. 40). Cameron's reading shows a Dickinson struggling with Christian orthodoxy, but here, as elsewhere, I see Dickinson appropriating it for her own, very personal, purposes. She needs renunciation, however, painful, as a form for survival.

27. *Letters*, II, #391, p. 508.

28. "The terms of grace were no less than the rejection of the self that the self be—to use another term Emily Dickinson took from Puritan theology—'justified' . . .," Sherwood, p. 168.

29. Keller, p. 95.

30. Webster, p. 411.

5. "Costumeless Consciousness"

1. Both Karl Keller and Robert Weisbuch concur regarding this crucial matter of the religious vocabulary, especially as it is used for heaven and eternity. "Crucifixion, the dust of the grave, resurrection, judgment, eternity, immortality—the familiar language is sufficiently pliable to set up a fruitful tension between traditional meanings and her own," observes Weisbuch (p. 82). Keller is even more emphatic. "The conservative terms are used but the conservative intent is cancelled out, making the assertion of herself possible. . . . The result is a homemade religion to suit her: the old terms are made to mean their opposites; the rituals are stolen and deritualized; the sacred is desecrated; the forms are reformed. She has subsumed the received and sustained her heretical desires by stealing terms to name her private heresy" (pp. 290–91).

2. *Letters*, III, #827, p. 779.

3. *Letters*, II, #319, p. 454.

4. Weisbuch, p. 129; Cameron, pp. 4, 5; Gelpi, *The Tenth Muse*, p. 265.

5. Cameron, pp. 9, 3.

6. *Letters*, III, #785, p. 750.

7. Weisbuch, p. 85.

8. *Letters*, III, prose fragment 99, p. 926; *Letters*, II, #288, p. 430.

9. Cameron, p. 10.

10. *Letters*, II, #280, p. 424.

11. *Letters*, II, #555, p. 612.

12. Weisbuch, p. 97.

13. Ibid., p. 103.

14. Anderson, p. 277; Weisbuch, p. 84.

15. Anderson, pp. 277, 276.

16. Ibid., p. 276.

17. Anderson's interpretations seem a little farfetched, and even he admits to some floundering when he tries 1) "The 'Disk' in the baffling final image would then become the moon, controlling the tides in their 'Schedule' by some mysterious force"; or 2) "The image she uses here . . . is the well

known one of the setting and the rising sun. . . . No matter how deep its 'Disk' plunges into the earth, or sea, this is the necessary condition for its rising again, on a 'Schedule' that is 'Deep' in the sense of being profound, since it is the absolute measure of time" (pp. 276, 277).

6. "I'm ceded–I've stopped being Theirs"

1. Homans, pp. 162–214.
2. Cody, p. 438.
3. To Suzanne Juhasz, 31 August 1981.

INDEX TO POEMS CITED